T0194344

Broken

A Widow's Memoir

ANGIE KAUFFMAN

WESTBOW
PRESS®
A DIVISION OF THOMAS NELSON
& ZONDERVAN

WestBow Press books may be ordered through booksellers or by contacting:

WestBow Press
A Division of Thomas Nelson & Zondervan
1663 Liberty Drive
Bloomington, IN 47403
www.westbowpress.com
1 (866) 928-1240

Scripture quotations are taken from the Holy Bible, New Living Translation, copyright ©1996, 2004, 2015 by Tyndale House Foundation. Used by permission of Tyndale House Publishers, Inc., Carol Stream, Illinois 60188. All rights reserved.

ISBN: 978-1-9736-6410-9 (sc)
ISBN: 978-1-9736-6409-3 (e)

Library of Congress Control Number: 2019906227

Print information available on the last page.

WestBow Press rev. date: 6/5/2019

To my family, friends, and community, without whose help I would have never been able to get through this difficult time in my life.

To my daughters, who have served as my earthly stability through all of the frustration and sadness.

To my God, who has comforted me and worked to give me wisdom for the coming days.

Contents

Foreword

There is an ancient Japanese form of art called Kintsugi that dates back to the 15th century when Japenese shogun Ashikaga Yoshimasa sent a cracked tea bowl back to China to be repaired. When it came back after being repaired, the shogun was dismayed to find that it had been mended with very unattractive metal staples. This motivated him to find a more pleasing way of repairing vessels. He invented the art of fixing broken pottery with a special lacquer dusted with powdered gold, silver, or platinum. Beautiful seams of gold shimmered in the cracks of ceramic ware, giving a unique appearance to the piece. This method of repair celebrates each vessel's unique history by emphasizing its fractures and cracks instead of hiding or disguising them. Often this ancient art form makes the original piece even more beautiful than it was before, revitalizing it to new life. The Japanese philosophy of wabi-sabi came into being in order to describe this art form, calling for seeing beauty in the flawed or imperfect. I desire to be that vessel. Yes, I know that I am daily tried and make mistakes. There are events in my life that have broken my spirit, but I know that God desires for me to depend on him to mend my broken parts internally and see the beauty of what he can do with my life. What matters is that I take my heartaches and use them as opportunities to bring glory to him!

A Day I Will Never Forget

Monday morning started out as usual. It was a beautiful, sunny morning. I woke up and pulled my devotional book out. It was a really interesting excerpt about a Japanese art form where they take and fix broken pottery. They do not just glue the pieces back together. They actually fill the cracks with gold, silver, or platinum. I imagined how gorgeous that must have been. Then, I saw a picture of it and it was stunning! I was reminded by God of how beautiful someone could be when they go through situations in their lives where they are broken and they are put back together again. After I said my prayers and did a load of laundry, I woke up my daughters and husband so that they could get ready for the day. My husband was very apologetic about not being able to spend any alone time together the night before and I reassured him that it was okay and that we had the "rest of our lives." I kissed him good-bye for the day and he left for work. I took the girls to school that morning and wished them a great day. Then, I set off to my worksite in another town about forty-five minutes away.

Before starting class, I remembered that I needed some medicine refilled from the local pharmacy. So, I texted my husband to see if he could pick it up during his lunch break. His reply was that he couldn't today. "Do you have enough to get you through until tomorrow? I may not be able to get by there since I'm doing taxes for my lunch and everything…" Huh? I thought. I texted back, "That's okay. No problem." I taught class that morning and was just about to start my afternoon class when I received a very strange telephone call. The person on the other end of the line said who she was. I thought that this was one of the secretaries at my daughters' school. But, then she told me that she was one of our neighbors in our subdivision. Then, the street sweeper got on the phone and told me who he was and that I might want to get home as soon as I could. Perplexed, I asked him what the problem was. He handed the phone to another person who told me that he was "Detective so and so..." with the police department and that I needed to make arrangements to come home as soon as possible. He said that there had been an incident. I asked him what kind of incident. The line was silent. I questioned him further, asking him if it was about my daughter who I knew had an out of town tennis match that day. I asked him about my other daughter who was at school as well as about my mother and grandma. He said that it was not about any of them. I told him, "You might as well tell me what is going on or I'm going to cry all the way home." He proceeded to tell me to stay right where I was and that he would send a police escort to come and get me from the school. I said okay and hung up.

I walked into my classroom and told my students that something had happened; I didn't know what, and that I was going to have to go home. I hugged one of my students who just happened to be one of my dearest friends and burst into tears. She immediately began pray. After she prayed, I apologized for crying and she told me that now was the time to do the ugly cry. Whatever the situation was at home, I needed to be able to be strong enough to get my daughters through whatever had happened. It was almost like the Holy Spirit had already told her what had happened. After waiting forty-five minutes like the cop had told me to, I went ahead and left the school. I called my mom and told her that I had gotten a strange phone call and that I was coming home because there had been some sort of incident. She said that she would call around to see what was going on and then she would call me back. I got into my car and started driving. She called me back and told me that something had happened. I asked her, "What is it? Is somebody dead?" She said that, yes, it was my husband. He had shot himself. Confusion went all through me as tears streamed down my face. "Why would he do this to us?" I asked my mom. She told me that she did not know. She told me that she did not know where exactly that it had happened, but that it was close to our house. She also told me that she was standing next to a policeman and then told him that she was talking to me. I asked her to tell the policeman that I was going to stop at the nearest store that I came to and wait for them to come and get me.

While I was waiting in that parking lot on that scorching day, I remember feeling like I was having an out of body experience. I couldn't even believe that any of this was happening to me! This was not something that typically happened to families like mine. We were not dysfunctional! My husband was a Christian. Why would he resort to something like this? Was there something that I said or did to cause him to want to hurt himself? Everything was so surreal. When the policeman and his partner arrived, I turned the car around and told him that I would be happy to follow them home. He told me that he would feel more comfortable if I hopped into the passenger seat and allowed him to do the driving. So, I did. I kept turning everything over and over in my mind on the way home and asking why the policeman did not just tell me what was going on. I know that it must have been standard protocol, but it really was not fair to keep the details of what was going on from me. The policeman that was driving really had the gift of gab. He tried to keep me calm by asking me questions about my career. While we were conversing, my pastor called me and asked me where I was. I told him that I was on the way home and he asked me where they were taking me. I told him that I did not know. I was not sure if they were going to take me to the site where it all happened or if they were taking me home.

I remember feeling like I was going to throw up as we came into town because I thought that I was going to have to identify my husband's body. They wound up taking me home instead and there were people there waiting for me. My pastor was waiting there as well. I went into the house and found my mother and sister. Everyone else was rushing around cleaning everything. I was partly grateful, but really ashamed that my house was so messy. Why in the world would he have chosen a Monday to do this? My house was always a wreck after the weekend on the first day of the week. Plus, Monday is just an awful day to get bad news! Stupid funny, I know, but true. I had not planned for all of this…I was so shocked that I could not even cry. I went back outside to greet my pastor and some really close friends who were standing around. The coroner came up and I immediately grabbed whoever's hand was closest. He told me the specifics around the incident, where they found him, who found him, and that they had ruled it a suicide. He asked me which funeral home that I wanted to use and I told him.

When that conversation ended, my really good friend who was on the worship team with me just grabbed me up like a ragdoll and hugged me. He said, "I'm so sorry, sister. We'll be right here. We're not going anywhere." I don't remember being hugged like that since my dad was alive. He was this big, burly guy who had a heart like a teddy bear. This friend of mine has always reminded me so much of my dad, but he's closer to my age. After he hugged me, my pastor's wife (another worship team family member) rushed up to me and just scooped me into her arms. "This is terrible, Angie. I can't believe that this happened." As I went from person to person who was there, people from my church; people from momma's church; people from down the street; I can only remember feeling numb. I felt lost. What in the world were we going to do? How were we going to be able to keep this house? Were we even going to be able to keep the house?

The evening went on just like that. It was about two o'clock in the afternoon at that time. My pastor's wife and sister were running around like chickens with their heads cut off doing stuff. By four o'clock, different people had brought anything from paper products to pizza to cokes to desserts. We were in no way in need of food. Then, I thought of my youngest daughter. She was at my Momma's house with Grandma and did not know yet. I felt like I needed to be the one to tell her and prepare her for all of this. I prayed all the way out to Momma's. When I got out there and found her, I found the gentlest way that I knew how to tell her. All she could ask was, "Why Momma?" I told her that I did not know and that there would probably be a lot of questions in the next few months or years that I would not know the answers to. But, I did know that we were not going to turn away from God because of this experience and that all that we could do was stick close together, pray, and talk as much as necessary to keep the lines of communication open. We sat together and cried for the longest time and then she popped up and went over to the computer. "What'cha doing?" I asked. "I'm googling some funny jokes so that I can make you feel better," she said. I smiled and told her that all I needed right now was her and her funny personality to cheer me up. To tell the truth, I was more worried about she and her sister than I was about myself.

My oldest daughter was in the middle of a tennis match and I was hoping that no one had broken the news to her yet because that would have just ruined her playing abilities on the court. As it turns out, the recreation director in our town had gotten word of what happened and he came by the house later to tell me that he had called the coach and asked him not to tell her yet or pull her off of the court. He thought that would have been my wishes and he was right! My youngest daughter got into the car and we rode over to the house. By then, even more people had arrived. I was both overwhelmed and relieved to be engulfed in the love of my family and friends. What I thought would be a very awkward situation turned out to be somewhat comfortable because everyone was all over the place in the house eating and visiting with one another. That was the way that my husband would have wanted it. My associate pastor worked himself silly trying to arrange things and did not leave until nearly eight o'clock that evening. It really meant a lot to me for him to stay. He took the time to minister to me. His parents had been killed in previous years in an airplane crash unexpectedly and he had a lot of perspective to give. He finally said, "I really better be getting home. Harriet doesn't even know where I am!"

When my oldest daughter came home, she got out of the van with tears pouring down her face. "It's all my fault, Mom. I was always so difficult with him." I told her that it was not her fault. My husband obviously was in a very dark place that no one else knew about. I took her to her room and we talked for a few minutes. As we were talking, all of her cousins banged on the door and wanted to spend time with her. The cousins were a God send for both of the girls. Spending time with them really relieved a great deal of stress and it made things lighter for the girls and everyone. There were teenagers and children running everywhere, but that was just the way that I wanted it.

People did not wind up leaving until nearly eleven thirty that night. And then, I don't think that anyone left us alone twenty-four/seven for about two weeks. I mean, people spent the night with us. People came over constantly to check on us. They handled all of the food and cleaning. I was astounded at the outpouring of love from our church and then the rest of the community as well. It was amazing how our town supported us through the entire experience. They sent cards, flowers, money, money, money, and food! I don't think we would have survived financially had it not been for people's generosity and my mom allowing us to stay at her house. It was like the Holy Spirit had already hovered over my town and was preparing people for all of this. My sister was particularly strong. She took care of all of the administrative details for everything. When we went places to talk to people, she was always there. When I did not have the presence to think of specific things to say or questions to ask, she was right on top of things. I don't remember thinking clearly for about a month. I felt like I was in a fog.

The reason that I chose to write about my experiences regarding this event in my life was because I wanted other widows, widowers, and others who have lost loved ones to know that they were not alone even if it is just the death of a relationship or a marriage. All of the feelings that a person experiences in the wake of a death are overwhelming, frustrating, and excruciatingly sad. From what I have gone through thus far, there doesn't seem to be a specific order that these feelings put themselves in and a person doesn't just get through one of the feelings and graduate to the next. It's like a person goes through one feeling one day, another the next, and then the last on yet another day. Then, he or she just jumps from one feeling to the next in no particular order in order to subconsciously survive through the grieving process. This happened to me as I began to handle all of the affairs concerning my husband's estate, the finances, and everything else that I was responsible for. This book is a compilation of journal entries that describe various experiences that I had following my husband's death. They are in no particular order from day to day. My desire is for this book to help you feel that you are not alone and that there is hope. There are funny parts to all of these experiences which I hope will make you smile. Finally, I hope that, even though your heart is broken, you can begin to see how God can put all the pieces back together again, perhaps making you even more beautiful than you were in the first place.

Journal Entry #1 Private Viewing

• • •

PRIVATE VIEWING

There was the day that we went to the funeral home to make sure that everything was set for the viewing in the evening. I had my sister with me along with my two pastor friends. I was unsure whether or not I was going to be able to look at my husband because I did not know the circumstances around his death. Those were still questions that I had not had answered by law enforcement. I mean, I knew that he shot himself and I knew that the damage must have been pretty bad, but I did not know the extent of the damage. A part of me was afraid to look at him even after being fixed up by the mortician because I was afraid that the image of him lying there would be indelibly ingrained in my memory. Just like my counselor told me, you can't "undo" a picture in your mind after you've already seen it. I had pretty much decided to let the men who I chose as my pastors for the funeral decide whether or not it would be best for me to look at him. When they came out of the room that my husband was lying in, they said that he looked okay and that it would not be traumatic, but that he did not look like himself; not that anyone who is dead looks like themselves, but anyway. My sister, who had gone into protective mode, had already decided that she was going to advise me not to go in to see him before we even got to the funeral home.

I decided that I would not look directly at my husband, but that I would ask the funeral home director if there was a heavy veil that he could cover his face and shoulders with so that I could at least touch his hands and talk to him. His hands were so pale and hairy. He was also unnaturally skinny. I didn't remember them looking like that, but I needed to remember that there was no life in them now. When my husband was alive, he was very tan, had dark eyes and hair, a cute ruddy complexion on his face, and the prettiest hands you have ever seen. He was also a "haus", meaning that he had broad shoulders and was not a skinny man, but was muscular and very healthy. Knowing all of this coupled with the fact that I had not been told all of the details around my husband's death, Satan began to sneak in and try to tell me, "You didn't see it. You don't know that he killed himself. He could have faked his own death. He could be miles away on a beach in Tijuana drinking cocktails with some trollop because he didn't want to be with you and the girls." I tried to shake it off, but it began to eat at me. I also had thoughts like, "I wonder if he was part of some secret organization or part of a drug ring. Or what if he was actually murdered?"…so many questions.

The casket that we chose was this stately greyish navy color with very little shine. We tried to choose the most masculine one that they had. It was all put composed, organized, and ready for visitation at 6:00 p.m. My husband was a very good-looking, well put together man. We would eventually choose to close the casket for the visitation and lay a beautiful blanket of red roses with woodsy cedar, tiny dark blue flowers, and baby's breath on top of the casket. It was the last time that I would see or feel his hands. How sad. As I touched his hands and straightened his suit, I asked out loud, "Honey, why did you do this? I just don't understand." Then, I began to tear up. I forced myself to swallow back the tears as I went back over to the loved ones that were waiting for me. The pastor of my church told me that the police had given the funeral home director some of the personal affects that my husband had had in his pockets (his license, credit cards, and business card case). I was shown a small note that my husband had typed and inserted into the mother-of-pearl business card case that I had given him for Christmas. The note reflected some things that he had been talking to me about at home like the fact that his equipment at work was always breaking and that his medicine was screwed up. One other thing that the note said was "critical mass." What was that? One pastor that I had chosen who just happened to be my youth pastor from growing up said, "You know, some people feel like when everything seems to be going wrong in their lives, they consider it to be a critical mass."

"Okay," I thought, perplexed. Clearly, this had been premeditated and he had been contemplating these thoughts for a while or he would have just written the note out. Another thing that I wondered was if he had just been told by the doctor that he actually had a critical cancerous mass. But, that would have shown up on the autopsy and it was not reported. Another question that I had was why the note was not hand written. Even though it was typed very neatly, the grammar in the note was not nearly what my husband would have used and the verb usage was all wrong which would have driven him crazy if he had read it out loud. What in the world happened? Did he really just go temporarily insane or did someone else actually type the note? While we were standing around talking, one of the members of the funeral home team came up to me and asked me to proof the program that they had printed for the evening. I was flabbergasted to see a picture of my husband on the front cover where he was at some sort of fun-run fundraiser with the civic club that he belonged to with a track suit on and one of those neck-cooler froggy things around his neck! Oh, this will never work, I thought. When I spoke with the lady about it, she said that that was the profile picture that he had on his social media, so that was why she decided to put it on there. She said that they had already printed several hundred copies of it (this is after we have given her a laundry basket full of pictures in frames that she could have chosen from...hmmm). What?! I looked at her and said, "Umm...we've got to do something else." So, she left the room to see what she could do to help us. It was during that time that I looked at my sister and asked her, "Now, how are you going to handle this?" This was somewhat humorous because my sister had taken care of everything that included administrative tasks and I just looked to her to keep everything together. I couldn't think for myself at the time. When the lady came back, my sister asked her if she had something more formal from the pictures that we had provided her. She invited us to come to the back room where all of the pictures were located. We chose to splice one of our wedding photos so that he could be seen in a formal suit and they agreed to print several more programs with that picture on it. Problem solved. I was still in fog mode at this time. Although I had questions, I wasn't all too consumed with getting answers to why my husband committed suicide at this point. All I knew was that my best friend was gone and that he wasn't coming back. I was also wondering how in the world I was going to hold it together for who was coming for the visitation that evening.

Journal Entry #2 The Visitation
• • •
THE VISITATION

My former boss who had recently retired from our program had come to the house and left a slew of dress clothes to wear to the visitation and funeral while we had been gone to the funeral home. She knew that I wasn't a "suit princess" and that I might need something very tailored to wear. That was so thoughtful of her! She had such great taste and, the suits, oh my gosh! I guess she must have known that I, a lowly teacher of twenty years, did not have a huge repertoire of suits. She was right. One of my best friends who I have worked out with for years was at the house when I got back and I tried on several of the outfits for them to let them help me decide what to wear. We settled on a silk black jumper with a tailored jacket for the visitation. For the funeral, I would wear one of my grandma's pretty dresses; a black pin-striped straight dress with a scooped neck that zipped up the back. Very stately. You may be thinking, "Grandma's dress? Ugh!" What you need to know is that my grandma was a very sharp dresser. Everything that she wore, even though she was in her 90's at the time, was always very smart looking. In fact, I tended to received more compliments on clothes that my grandma gave me than when I wore things that I bought myself!

I stood there at the mirror putting on my make-up and struggling because I kept crying everything off that I had just put on. I couldn't seem to get myself together. Then, one of my closest friends came in. She and I grew up together because our dads were both coaches. This was a big surprise! I didn't know that she was coming. She has a way of calming me down and making everything better. With her help, I was able to calm down long enough to be able to keep my makeup on. Mom came over to pick all of us up to take us over to the funeral home. When I got there, my husband's family (all seven siblings, their spouses and children; he was the oldest of all of them; his parents) was already there. We all agreed that keeping the casket closed was the best decision. They brought all sorts of food for the family to snack on in the conference room. I wasn't all that hungry. I just wanted this night to go swiftly. At six o'clock, people started coming in for visitation. I have never seen so many people in my life. They just kept coming! I mean, I knew that my husband was a very charismatic individual and that he was popular in the community, but I had no idea that he knew so many folks. Given that he has a large family, there were several of his relatives that came to pay their respects. I was floored at the delicate and respectful way that they approached me. Some relatives from his extended family had never been that kind to me before in the total eleven years that we had been married. I was his second marriage and many of them did not believe that I was the right pick for him at the time or that it was right for him to remarry after divorce given their beliefs.

Despite the sadness of the occasion, the Holy Spirit must have known that I needed some comic relief. There were so many people waiting outside, I mean, around the block (yes, that's what I said!) that my sister kept prompting me to keep the line moving. I'm serious, I've never seen anything like it! I was overwhelmed with sadness, love from relatives, and thankfulness that people were so loving toward us. As a moment of unexpected humor, there was one person who came up to me and all I could think of because of his short stature was that he reminded me of one of those oompa loompa characters from that movie, Charlie and the Chocolate Factory. Moments later, I could have sworn that Weird Al Yankovich came up and hugged me. I promise I'm not going crazy. That is exactly what these people reminded me of. Thinking back, I really feel like that was the Holy Spirit trying to comfort me in strange and unexpected ways. The last few visitors came in and left at nine p.m. that evening. The visitation was set to last from six to eight! Afterwards, the families sat in the conference room, ate and talked for a while. We also went into the visitation room and took a look at the multitude of flowers and plants that had been sent to see who they were from. I can't ever remember feeling so sad, but so comforted in God's arms at the same time. It was an amazing, heart-wrenching, overwhelming time.

Journal Entry #3 The Funeral

• • •

THE FUNERAL

As I recount all of the events leading up to the funeral and the stages of planning, all I can think of are the wonderful times with friends and family who never left our side. I can remember sitting around the table with my mom, sister, pastors and their wives planning the service from where we would have the meal for his huge family to the specific food that would be served. I also remember discussing what we would do if we had an overflow of guests. I had pretty much decided that I didn't know what we were going to do if that happened. In my husband's home church that he grew up in, if there was an overflow of guests at services, the extra people would simply go down and sit in a finished, air-conditioned basement where the service was piped down there for everyone else to watch. Well, our church did not offer that option. Little did I know that the Holy Spirit had already prompted my pastor on the matter. When I brought it up to him, he said, "Got it covered, Ang...We will just put overflow crowd in extra education rooms in the church and pipe the service in through television monitors. No problem." Amazing. Problem solved.

As far as the meal, I had already decided that I wanted a special dish that was one of my favorites to be served-good comfort food-for me....I just wanted spicy chicken tetrazzini, salad, homemade yeast rolls, sweet tea and dessert. Not a problem. I had a friend who was a whiz at catering who had all of it covered before I could even get it out of my mouth. As far as how the service would be conducted, I knew that my husband would have wanted a mix of the two cultures between the families. His family was from an Amish-Mennonite background and I wanted his heritage to be represented equally in the service. I chose a few hymns that I wanted to be sung and then left the rest of those choices for his sisters. The last thing that needed to be worked out was the graveside ceremony. In Mennonite culture, they do things a little differently for closure purposes. Instead of allowing the funeral home to dig the hole that the body would be lowered into, members of the Mennonite church dig it themselves. There's usually a coordinator and he instructs those assigned as pallbearers as to exactly how it is to be done. I allowed my husband's family to completely plan that part because I knew that is what he would have wanted.

On the day of funeral, we all piled in the car (me, my daughters, and my mom) and drove to the church. The funeral was supposed to start at 11:00 a.m. We drove up at 10:30 and the parking lot was full! There were so many people milling around that I told momma that we were going to have to walk around to the back. When I got around to the back of the church, my preacher's wife grabbed me and hugged me. She was a bundle of nerves. "Oh, you look so beautiful! I just don't know how in the world you're going to get through this! What can I do for you?" I remembered that I had left my purse at the funeral home the night before and I asked her if she could find me some lipstick. She looked at me like, "Funny request" and then went running to find some. I walked into the back education building and saw all of my husband's family in one of the rooms. My father in law gently hugged me and said, "You don't have an earthly father anymore, so let me be that to you from now on." Oh, how sweet! I thanked him and hugged him back. As I was greeting my husband's siblings and mother, my preacher's wife rushed back into the room and brought me lipsticks. She said, "Ok, I have mauve and I have this rose color. I took the mauve and kissed her on the cheek." She later told me the story about how she acquired the lipstick and it was a side splitter. I digress, but let me share it with you. She went into the sanctuary and asked one of the funeral directors who was a lady who happened to have a scratchy voice if she knew where my purse was. "I thought that Mr. Bobby was bringing it back to the church this morning. Angie left it at the funeral home last night," the pastor's wife said. In her raspy voice, she said very loudly, "I don't know where Bobby or her purse is right now!" At that point, about fifty people turned around to see what the racket was! My preacher's wife was beginning to get rattled. She turned around and locked eyes with Angela. I sing with both of them on Sunday mornings on the worship team for church. Angela asked her what was wrong. She said, "Angie needs lipstick!" Angela went rooting through her purse and brought out all the lipsticks that she had. So, thank you, Angela and Stacey for the lipstick. Bosom buddies!

It was time for us to line up to walk into the sanctuary for the service. Seriously….moment of truth. It just got very real. I grabbed both of my girls' hands and we started walking. I have never had that many people looking at me at one time in my entire life. The service was beautiful. Both of our daughters held it together so well! I was so proud of them. In a traditional Mennonite funeral, there are hymns sung acapella. I had not even thought about the fact that my mom and sister had never experienced that (as well as many people in our community). All I could think about at the moment that I was sitting there was how comforting it all was. The beautiful harmonies from the voices just resonated with me; ministered to me. When we got into the funeral limousine, my mom told my mother-in-law that it was like she was in heaven. She had never heard anything like it. The sound of all of those people singing together was so full and complete. I had always been so glad that I received the opportunity to get to know my husband's heritage, but now I was doubly glad because my mother, sister, and entire community had gotten a taste of it as well. You wouldn't believe the people who personally connected with me after that day to express those thoughts.

We rode together to the grave sight. Normally, I would have worried about how everything went, but I really had no worries about it. I had this peace that I had chosen wisely and that this was probably going to be the most beautiful part of the entire day. The pallbearers that I had chosen were all there. Everything was set up. You see, in my husband's heritage, the pallbearers actually dig the hole and lower the body down into the grave themselves. This allows for people to throw flowers into the grave, shovel dirt, whatever they need to do in order to get closure. I wanted to do that for Roland. I didn't expect it to make such an impact on the community or my immediate family. There were people who reached out to me later and told me that it was the sweetest, most meaningful graveside service that they had ever attended. There was an acapella youth choir that stood behind the family singing hymns for comfort. A sermon was preached right there at the cemetery and then family members were invited to shovel dirt, sing, hug, and pay their respects.

My mom and sister were truly impacted by all of the things that they observed from the service. They both reached out to relatives from Roland's family during that service and asked them if they could shovel dirt or go up to the grave and pay their respects. But, they didn't want to go by themselves. So, Roland's mom went with my mom and one of his sisters went with my sister.

We got back into the car and were taken to the church for the meal. Everyone was already there, so it was like, "I'm home, everybody." The sanctuary had been totally converted into like a fellowship hall with round tables everywhere. People could go through the kitchen to get their food and then an entire room had been set up with desserts that people could go through, compliments of many of the Mennonite aunts and cousins. Yum! The drinks were in the vestibule of the church. It was so organized! God truly had his hand on everything-I knew it! What could have been a really strained, uncomfortable situation with family because of the way that Roland died turned out to be so smooth and supported by all. God's love transcends every potential dissention and diffuses all confusion.

Journal Entry #4 Legal Matters

• • •

LEGAL MATTERS

A few days after the funeral dealings died down, I began to realize the need to look at the financial upheaval that had been caused by my husband's death. I first spoke with my lawyer, establishing a living will and discussing assets. The only asset that I was privy to at the time was the investment account that was in my husband's name, so I drew it out (with penalty, of course). I then started with the credit cards, both of which were in Roland's name. I called the card services of both of the companies to see what the balance was on the cards. I told them what had happened, reminded them that the cards were not in my name, and asked them what it was going to take to clear me of those charges. I wound up having to fax them death certificates. I continued for months to receive threatening letters and calls from both companies about paying off the balance. My lawyer, who I had spoken with about the matter, told me not to worry about it; that they couldn't do anything to me. One day, there was a woman who called wanting to ask me a ton of questions regarding the credit card account including what my social security number was. I politely told her that my attorney would be glad to answer any questions that she might have about the credit card account. I said, "His name is..... and his number is 229-924-..... Oh! And, ma'am, what is your social security number?" She indicated that she was not going to give that to me. To which I replied, "Well, what makes you think I'm going to give you mine! Good day, ma'am." I hung up. Eventually, they stopped calling. Whew!

Then, there was the matter of pursuing life insurance money. There were two different companies that, when I sent them the necessary paperwork, and after repeating my story an exhausting amount of times over a period of weeks, finally sent me letters stating that they were denying my request because there was a clause in my husband's policy that stated that it would not pay in situations such as suicide. That made me mad. Another thing that saddened me was that a prominent life insurance salesman came over to our house for a special meeting one day. He indicated that Roland had had an insurance policy with him, but that he had let it lapse. Now, I want to tell you that my sister was sitting across the table from this man. Given the protectiveness of my sister at the time, you'll begin to see where this story is going. The very southern gentleman said, "Well, unfortunately you are not eligible to receive the funds that your husband had in his account because he dissolved it. The account had $75,000 in it." Yes, we had chosen to dissolve the account with that company at one time because I was going through a dry spell with a job and we needed to cut corners anywhere that we could. My sister could see that I was about to tear up, so she quietly told him that she appreciated him coming by, but that we would have to talk about the matter at another time. He continued, "Yep. I sat there on that stool at his workplace one day and told him that he had better not let that policy lapse, and that he sure better not go and do something stupid like kill himself." That was the last straw. No joke; I really thought that my sister was going to crawl across the table and pinch his head off. She reiterated in a "not so whispery" voice that the meeting was over, but that we appreciated him taking the time to come by. Surprisingly, he found a way to scrape up a $300.00 check for us from the policy in order to ease our suffering. After he left, we prayed and I don't remember ever sobbing so hard that I slobbered ever in my lifetime, but I did that time. Another thing that needed to be resolved was the fact that we had a pop-up camper that we were still paying on. It was an $18,000 debt. I called the camper company and made a deal with the devil that I would be willing to totally surrender the camper up for auction in exchange for not having to pay the payments any longer. So, that nightmare went away for good.

What was good was that I began assuming responsibility for the bills again. I always helped my husband write the checks, but he usually handled all of the tough money situations. Luckily, he always made me aware of what he was doing and there were no surprises there. As I went through the finances, I began to realize that it was going to be extremely difficult on my salary to pay the bills along with the mortgage, which was sky high because we had had to refinance within the past five years. After much prayer, I decided to put the house on the market. As luck would have it, my Mom insisted that we come out and live with her for a while. So, I cut off all of the expenses to our house except for the water, electricity, and mortgage. There were times that I needed to go over there just to have some time to myself due to the fact that, although I loved living with my mom, life there could sometimes be a tad crowded. After the fact, though, I was glad that we went to live with Mom for six months. My grandma lived out there with her and it gave me the chance to spend the last several months of her life with her. Although she had begun to progress through the beginning stages of dementia, there were still wonderful talks and discussions where I gleaned so much wisdom from her. She passed away the December after we moved out of Mom's house.

As we began to go through the process of acquiring a realtor and show our house, it became strikingly clear that all of this was real and that my life was changing forever. My soul mate was not coming back. Oh, how I missed our talks on the back porch on rainy nights, laughing like crazy at television shows together, solving all of the problems of the world sitting in poolside chairs when we would go to the beach and the girls would be night swimming. He was truly my best friend. It was so heartbreaking that I was never going to get to rub my fingers over his sweet, tan face, look into his beautiful brown eyes, or enjoy his hunky body again. But, on the other hand, I was angry. I mean, he was the strongest Christian that I knew. What in life was so bad that he had to end his life? Did I make life that hard on him? Why did he make the choice to leave us? I remember in one of our early morning talks, my sister answered that question, making me realize that when he pulled the trigger, he wasn't thinking of anyone but himself. He just wanted to end whatever inner pain he was dealing with. That definitely put things into perspective for me. I remember looking at my pastor and his wife in horror halfway through the evening that he died, asking them, "How in the world am I going to explain this suicide thing to the girls when their dad had always told them that if someone killed him or herself, they went straight to hell?" And, to those who question this, I will say that my pastor explained to me that there are two schools of thought regarding suicide and eternity. One is that if someone kills himself, he would not have time to repent and ask forgiveness before he died. But, is there anywhere in the bible addressing suicide except for Judas? What the bible does say is that the only unpardonable sin is blasphemy (saying that there is no God). When people have the audacity to look at me with pity and say, "I'm so sorry that you can't be sure that you're ever going to see your husband again," I have to politely put them in their place by helping them understand that unless they have walked in these shoes, they will truly never understand the dynamics of what we have been through. I also remind them of the biblical statements that I made in the previous sentences because I have to believe that my husband has made things right with God and that everything is alright with him. I have to believe that he went temporarily insane. These things help give me peace of mind.

Now, let me tell you about selling my house. So, around October, the girls decided that they wanted to go camping. I rented a rickety cabin at Chehaw Park and we set off on our adventure. We had such a good time. Out of process of trial and error, I taught myself how to grill on a campfire and made hamburgers and vegetables. I was so proud of myself and I was hoping that Roland might be looking down from heaven smiling at me. When we got home, the girls and I talked and decided that it was time to move back home. No one had looked at the house in the past month. We were convinced that we were not going to be able to sell it, even after we fresh baked chocolate chip cookies and left them in the cake plate for showings several times in the past six months. We packed everything that we had taken to Mom's in trash bags. Let me stop and tell you that you can't imagine all of the things that you take to your Mom's when you are living with her. Oh my gosh! We got home, dumped our trash bags out on our beds as well as all of the dirty linens and clothes from our camping trip in front of the washer and dryer. Then, we got ready and went to school the next morning.

I was teaching my night class when I received a very interesting call. It was my realtor, asking if he could show my house at 7:00 p.m. on a Monday evening! I told him that they were welcome to come and look at our house. It was very lived- in and I was sure that they would feel comfortable because it was a complete wreck! After all, nobody was going to put in an offer on our house anyway. I got off of the phone, turned to my students and told them what the call was about and looked at them like I was very perplexed. One of students said, "Miss Angie, that's God. It's just too weird and there's no logical explanation for it." Do you know that those people looked at three different houses that night and ours was the only one that they put in an offer on? Amazing! Granted, the selling process was drawn out about a month longer than usual because I had to counter-offer a couple of times, but the house got sold. In the meantime, I had looked at another house right down the street from my sister. Going under contract with my buyer enabled me to be able to start the buying process for this other house where my mortgage payment was going to be $400.00 less than the old house. There were a few glitches. My buyer wanted to go ahead and get in to do renovations early, forcing me out. So, the guy that owned the house that I was buying offered to rent the house to me until the closing date for us! The only problem was, he would not get with the realtor to say exactly when we could move in. So, we were all but last minute finding out if we were going to actually be able to move on the day that we had planned. I mean, 9:00 in the morning of the moving day was when the realtor called me and gave me the go-ahead! Little did I know that the cavalry was coming.

My entire church showed up at my house to help us pack up and move on that day. One of the guys who raced cars in a nearby town on the weekends offered his huge trailer and then another couple of guys brought their pick-up trucks. We were moved in by the end of the day. Women even brought sandwiches. Do you have any idea how much money that saved us? Although I offered to pay the rent at closing, the seller would never take it. He also left lots of building materials that I could use at his house when they moved out that I was able to use while renovating the house that I bought. I cannot tell you how many times within the year of Roland dying that people allowed God to use them to do miracles. Men in the church were constantly asking me if they could do anything from cutting the grass to fixing things around the house. The preacher and his wife came and helped me put my bed up. I bought a new one when I moved and sold most of the furniture. It was too hard to have the old bedroom set in my room. I was determined that we were going to have a fresh start without any extra sadness on top of the how we were already grieving. Between people in the community and my brother-in-law setting up a Go Fund Me account on Facebook sending us enough money, we were able to pay off the funeral in full, the realtor, the down payment on our house, and all of our medical bills! God is good ALL the time! Mark my word. I could just tell story after story.

I guess I just feel for those who lose loved ones and are strapped with all of the responsibilities of taking care of all of these financial matters. I could almost act as a grief counselor to guide people on what order to tackle all of those challenges. I don't want people to feel lost. I want them to know what to do to get things in order when someone that they are close to dies. It's hard enough losing them, not to mention having to handle all of the financial aspects of the death.

Journal Entry #5 Graduate School

• • •

GRADUATE SCHOOL

There were questions that went through my mind as I was sitting at the kitchen table on the evening of Roland's death as to whether or not I was going to finish my doctoral degree. I only had two semesters left. Before I even got out of my mouth what I was thinking, someone at the table piped up and asked, "So, Angie...I guess this probably means that you are going to quit doctorate school now." All of a sudden, something went through me and I said, "Of course not. I'm going to finish. More than anything, I want to finish now." Little did I know, there were still many challenges ahead of me. Needless to say, planning presentations, technology and practicing for presentations were a struggle at Mom's house. It was just so busy all of the time. So, many times I would retreat back to the old house to be able to have the presence of mind to study and prepare for presentations. Other times that I needed to prepare, I would just practice at school when I did not have classes by talking to an empty room full of desks or walk down the hall talking to myself when I knew no one else was there between classes. About two weeks after all of this happened, my closest doctoral professor emailed me, expressing condolences from the dissertation committee. I really never intended for him to find out what had happened because I did not want anybody feeling so sorry for me that they would just let me slide through the last stages of doctoral school. The girls and I were already under a microscope with people watching and talking about what happened. That would just compound the situation. I picked up the phone and called my lead professor. He asked me all kinds of questions, including, "Well, do you want to continue this?" Without hesitation, I said, "Yes, there is no reason to quit now. I am so close!" I realized later that continuing my education was probably the best way that I could have begun the healing process for myself because I thrive when I am busy and when I am writing. Might I say that I was truly blessed to have the professor that helped me with my dissertation. I do not think that I could have ever had a more patient person to help me. He knew how to motivate me, challenge me, and encourage me despite my super high maintenance personality. I was his first doctoral student and I was sure that he had promised himself that he would never do this again!

In most doctoral programs, a student has to do three presentations: first defense, defense proposal, and final defense. I had already passed my first defense before my husband died. I was now preparing to present my proposal. It was a longer presentation with much more information. I had to convince my committee that this research would be viable and that it would enhance the field of education in a positive way. I practiced until I was blue in the face. When I finally traveled to the university to meet up with my professors (because I was a transit/online student), I had my guns blazing. I was ready. I had prayed and practiced so hard! I arrived at the education department and my main professor (chair) asked me to come down to the second chair's office who was to help with the methodology of the dissertation (calculating numbers and results). As I entered his office, he invited me to come in and sit down. He proceeded to take his copy of my dissertation and go through it, asking me questions about how I planned to handle different parts of it. He also made suggestions on some changes that he would make on how I collected my data. I was flabbergasted! What?! I had my power point ready and everything and they did not want me to present it! I was in and out of there in thirty minutes. I am not joking. I would like to say that it seemed like they took it easy on me because of the tragedy that had just happened in my life, but they sure were not taking it easy on me in any other areas. My chair would shoot feedback to me online in the form of underlined paragraphs and comments that looked like a pig had died on the document. He would ask me questions like, "Where is the citation?" "What do you mean by this statement? It is unclear and hard to understand." "How do you know this?" "How do you plan on doing this part?" So many corrections....it drove me crazy! But, later I realized why he was grilling me so hard. It was because he wanted me to know that material backwards and forwards in order to truly defend the study that I was conducting. He did not want my presentations to be rote memorization. He wanted me to live, breathe, eat and sleep my study. He wanted me to get up there and "own" my presentation like I was the expert and no one knew as much about it as I did.

Anyway, I had promised myself that I would be drowning my sorrows or celebrating, either way, with Arby's on the way home regardless. So, off I went to get my roast beef sandwich, potato cakes, and milk shake with tears streaming down my face because I knew that everything that had just happened at the university had had God's hand on it. He truly meant for me to get this degree. That was encouraging because there were times that I would just stop and ask myself, "Why am I putting myself through this!" Confirmation. Period.

Now, my job was to go back home and take three months to contact all of the schools that I planned to survey, get permission to do my research through their superintendents, collect data, and then go through the process of analyzing all of it. I promise, it was not nearly that fast. It was a very long, arduous, harrowing process because public school people are so hard to reach! Then, when you reached them, you really wanted to establish a positive rapport with them so that they would feel safe with you doing research in their district. During this time, my chair was rather quiet, sitting back to see what I was going to bring back to him. By the time I had collected all of the data for the survey that I had set up, I learned that I had sent surveys out to a little over 1,000 teachers and gotten about 300 responses back. This was actually a pretty good sample, believe it or not.

It was time to get back in touch with my professor in order to begin the process of crunching all of these numbers according to the different variables in my study. I really do not want to go into all of the details because it would bore you and you would probably lay this book down, but I had to learn how to use a statistical software to plug in all of my data and variables. The software would then perform the calculations for me. All I had to do was my put in the different tests that I wanted to measure for and instruct the software to crunch those numbers as well. This was very difficult for me because writing I excel at, statistics I do not. I am not ashamed to say that YouTube videos, the graduate assistant saved me, and my colleague with whom we had stuck together throughout the entire three and half years of graduate school helped me make sense of it all because statistics were his jam! I was so confused on so many days, but I learned that if you look hard enough and ask enough questions with persistence, God will help you figure things out.

It was now time for me to create a power point for my final defense discussing the research, the reason that it was important, how I conducted it, on how many school districts, the sample, the results, and recommendations for further research. This would be a forty minute presentation. So, here I go in the Chevrolet Malibu puttering back up to the university for what I hoped would be the final time. My professor showed me to the meeting room when I got settled and I pulled up my power point. I began to practice to myself until all professors arrived. I gave my presentation, they grilled me with several questions, and then asked me to leave the room so that they could deliberate. There were a few questions that they asked me that I did not know how to answer. To which, I just gave my professor the "deer in the headlights" look and he ran interference for me. When I exited the room, I was so scared that I thought I was going to throw up. Feelings of discouragement were also washing all over me because they had asked me so many difficult questions, a few of them I could not answer. I just sat there in the lobby, students breezing by, praying (eyes closed), "God, I know that I have truly given all that I have. I do not have anything left. I poured my heart out in there. Whatever you choose to do, I know that it is your will and I will be okay with it."

My professor came back out after what seemed like an eternity and told me to step back into the meeting room. He extended his hand out to me and told me, "Congratulations Dr. Kauffman. Your study has been a success and your dissertation will be approved for publishing in the Columbus State University doctoral portal. I just stood back and said, "What did you just call me?" Then, it hit me. I had done it! They asked me to sit down; that there were still a few things about the study that needed to be altered (changed; fixed to be clearer for future dissertation students to read) in order for it to be officially approved for publishing and that I had two weeks to amend it and turn in the final copy. After the meeting when it was just me and my professor talking, he shook my hand and said, "I truly have never met anyone with as much grit and determination as you. Do not ever change." Those words meant so much to me! I made a beeline to Arby's and drove home. I could not wait to tell my Mom everything. Although I had lots of helps on this journey, she was my biggest cheerleader. During the next couple of weeks, I remember my dissertation chair going back and forth about twenty times with me receiving feedback in order to make sure that everything was written and formatted correctly. When he finally sent me an email where he had sent my dissertation to my doctoral advisor, I knew that I was completely finished. I just sat there and sobbed for I do not know how long. What a journey!

I am so glad that I took it because it developed me so much as a person. Before I was this shy person who had no speaking abilities whatsoever; a "Moses" if you will. I actually began my doctorate thinking that I had partially gotten into it because of the possible increase in pay. After a couple of years (and, yes, it takes between three to four years to earn a doctorate if you stay on track), I began to realize that it was not about the money at all. It was about a quest for knowledge and self-empowerment so that I could help empower others. Although I would rather sing in front of a crowd than speak on any day now, I really have no problem doing talks in front of large groups of people. I do not get nearly as nervous anymore. Trust me. Nothing is as scary as standing in front of a firing squad like a dissertation committee! If I could do that, I could do just about anything. I am a much more self-assured person now. But, going through doctoral school had a profound, humbling effect on me that I could never describe to you in words. I still had a long way to go, but I was just one step closer to being more like Jesus. Meek. Power under control. Never underestimate the power of a quiet woman who chooses her words wisely, prays, and who is directed by the Holy Spirit. You do not have to be loud and brassy to be powerful. Also, do not let people pat you on head and put you down because they think that you are a mouse just due to the fact that you a quiet soul. You are much stronger than people think you are. You do not have to tell them. Those that matter will see it. True power comes from within straight from the one who fills our holes when we are broken and heals us from the inside out.

Journal Entry #6 Fearless

• • •

FEARLESS

I really do not understand why people do not make it a point to go and see those who have lost loved ones, especially to suicide. They say, "Oh, I just would not know what to say." Are those statements made to actually honor the one who died, make viable excuses, or to protect themselves? I am so sorry, but I have to say that that is so lame. A slew of people came to see us when Roland died and those who really loved us did not even care about their personal reservations. They just came! I have a friend who was in the military who told me, "Well, I just had a lot of friends who were soldiers in my group who committed suicide while I was serving and I developed such an anger towards them because of wimping out while serving that I could not make myself come. I am sorry." Bull. There were so many things that I had to take care of when all of this happened that I did not have the luxury of saying, "Oh, I don't feel like facing that today. I'll just handle that next week." I didn't have the luxury of crawling into my closet and hiding out for six months because I had two wonderful jewels watching to see how their Momma was going to get through this. They needed a model to observe. We had to join hands, be strong for each other, and get through it. There were many times that I was so scared of the future, but I had to just take a deep breath, not think about it, and walk into the situation. There were also all of these baby Christians in the community who were watching to see how

I was going to handle this. I could not just turn my back on God. He's always been there for me. Why would I turn my back on him? If anything, we had to cling to God now more than ever. Right after Roland died and I saw how many people were trying to pour their love out on us, I realized that it wasn't just about "Angie, Roland's wife." People really did address us as "Angie and her girls." That became so personal and profound because I realized that a person can have such an impact on everyone that they come in contact with every day and not even realize it. It affects people and your Christian witness. Be very careful about how you live your life and the things that come out of your mouth. People are watching and listening.

Journal Entry #7 Investigator

• • •

INVESTIGATOR

While we were living with Mom, there were days when I needed to go back to the house to do some personal stuff or to just have a few minutes to myself. There were several days when I went back to the house to do some uninterrupted exercise that I would also do some personal investigating due to the fact that I was just so dissatisfied with what I had been told about the events surrounding Roland's death. Not to be negative, but law enforcement was not up on the top of my list when it came to giving needed information or answering questions regarding my love's death. In one case, I felt particularly patronized. When the assistant coroner came to the house (not the coroner who I personally knew...) to report what had actually happened, he said that it had been ruled a suicide. Roland was found in his car on a street close to our house with the motor running, music on, with blood running down the side of his face. Well, the mental pictures that I had in my mind did not match up with what he told me. So, after doing research (morbid, I know, but I needed answers), I could see that it is possible to have a gunshot wound to the chin and not totally obliterate the skull. What actually happened was that he shot himself in the chin and the bullet lodged in the back of his skull, therefore shattering it. According to the autopsy report, there was not an exit wound, which made his brain and the rest of the affected area swell profusely. I just had to look it up so that

I could see for myself since I chose not to see the body and I needed some beginnings of closure. Anyway, the assistant coroner treated me like, "Well, this little lady is so delicate today that she cannot take any other information that I give her (like the fact that the rest of the car was soiled, resulting in the insurance company having to replace every single bit of upholstery when they took it to be cleaned-that raised some questions in my head)." People so underestimate my level of strength as a person because I am a very laid back, quiet soul (eye roll).

Another situation that I remember not being satisfied with was when we went to the station to pick up his effects. I had a list of questions in my mind that I wanted to ask the officer who was there at the scene. When we sat down, I began to fire questions at him that I already knew the answers to just to see if he was going to tell the truth. Some of the questions that I asked were: Were his clothes soiled? Which hand did he have the gun in? Was the car running? Who was the first person who found the body? Why were they there? When they walked up, what did they report that they saw? His reply to most of the questions was, "Ma'am, I don't know the answer to those questions." To that, I retorted, "You were the officer at the scene, weren't you? It seems strange to me that you don't know the answers to those questions." So, you can see why there are reasons why I imagined that there could have been foul play. I immediately asked the funeral home director to obtain a copy of the autopsy and crime lab report for me to look at. I requested a toxicology report more than once. When I got to the funeral home to meet and talk with him about it, there was no toxicology report. I was ticked. The reason why I asked for it was that I had heard from one of Roland's painter friends that for about two weeks before he died, when he went in to buy paint, Roland acted like a zombie. I wondered if Roland was taking some kind of drug during the day that affected him, yet it had worn off by the end of the day. He did not act like a zombie at home in the evenings. I wanted to see if there was something in his system that may have been affecting his judgment when he died.

After I left the funeral home, I talked to my sister about my frustration. She said that, "Maybe the holy spirit just doesn't want you to know what happened right now." That was not a satisfying statement to me! When I got to the coffee shop where I was going to meet my daughters, I called the coroner and asked him where the toxicology report was. He said that the state patrol had decided not to do one. I asked why? He said that they just opted not to do one. "After I requested one multiple times?" I asked. Dead silence. Not an "I'm so sorry" or "I'll try to find something out for you." Nothing. I was livid! Now, I need to explain something. I mean no animosity toward law enforcement or local leaders. I back the blue to the hilt and I am not one to stir up trouble. What I would like for them to understand though is that, although I know and respect that they have to follow standard protocol, when they do not tell loved ones everything that they need to know, it really keeps people from getting the closure that they need. This is not just for the time surrounding the death, but for years! I felt like their viewpoint was that I was this little, young lady who couldn't handle the truth. The truth is, I'm a big girl with big girl panties and I can handle anything that you throw at me. Just tell me the truth! I know that I can't be the only person in this situation that feels that way. Again, let me reiterate that I respect the law enforcement in our county and in all counties. That's all that I'm going to say about it and I will not be going around and trashing law enforcement in our community because that is not the kind of person that I am, nor is it characteristic of the family that I come from. My grandpa was a law enforcement officer for his entire career, for goodness sake!

Anyway, let me get back to my house where I was exercising when I needed personal time to myself. When I would get finished working out, I would always search through drawers, under the bed, through my husband's closet, under the mattress, anywhere that I could think of that might give me more clues as to why he did what he did. When I would never find anything out, I would spiral and find myself on my knees, curled up on the floor, crying out to God to help me. "Please don't leave me, Holy Spirit. I need you desperately to help me through this. I know that there must be a reason that I'm not finding anything out that would help me understand. I know that you know what is best. Please help me to be content with the situation."

Many times when I would be driving, I would pray out loud and voice my thoughts. One time I felt the Holy Spirit whisper to me, "You met Roland when you were in a place in your life where you really needed exactly the kind of person that he was: funny, enthusiastic about his faith, attentive, a true gentleman. What you fail to see is that I was there before you met Roland. I was there the entire time you were with him. And I'm here now. I'm not leaving you. Here are the answers. There are none. You just have to trust me." Well, he certainly had the last word.

Journal Entry #8 Diamond Necklace

• • •

DIAMOND NECKLACE

On this day, the girls and I were on the way to the beautician. I reached up and accidentally broke a very precious necklace that my grandmother gave me when I turned sixteen. She took each diamond from her engagement ring and had a separate necklace with a pendant made for each one of us. The tradition was for her to give each of her granddaughters their special necklace when they turned sixteen. Well, I am now 45 years old and I have worn that necklace every day since I received it. Every once in a while, I break the chain and I find myself on the floor in tears trying to find the diamond because it is the last piece of my grandma on my mom's side that I have. So, I broke my necklace and had it all in my hand. I tried to give it to my oldest daughter who was sitting in the front passenger seat and she accidentally dropped it. I freaked out. When we arrived at the beautician, I sent them in and stayed outside to look for the necklace. So, picture it, both doors of the trailblazer are open and I'm crying, walking from side to side, trying to look for this necklace. Can you imagine what people who were driving by were thinking? After looking for about thirty minutes, I finally found it in the most unlikely place! Do you know where the plastic meets the carpet part of the car when you open the door? That's where it was. I was relieved, but I kept crying. How in the world did that necklace wind up in the door area when I gave the necklace to my daughter over the console of the car? It's a mystery to me.

I went inside, tear stained and raccoon faced, and sat down. I just did the ugly, loud cry right there in front of everybody. I didn't care. I can imagine that my beautician thought, "Oh, my goodness. She really is going crazy!" I have done that a couple of other times since and apologized to her. She is so understanding and sympathetic. It was not just because I had lost my necklace and found it. It was just a culmination of all of the headaches, heartache, confusion, and sadness that I was going through. I had a long way to go as far as healing.

Journal Entry #9 Dating 101

• • •

DATING 101

A little over two years have passed since Roland died and there is so much to share. Within the last six months, I just began to entertain the notion of dating again. After getting on a dating site, I quickly realized that dating now is quite different than it was twelve years ago. For one thing, texting seems to be the biggest mode of communication and I would just rather talk over the telephone or face to face. Men seem to be different than they were back then or maybe I just lucked up because I ran into Roland right off the bat and did not have to deal with guys that are what my girls call "players." You know, the guy who is not really interested in getting to know you as a person. They are just interested in physical relations. Well, that's not how I roll. I am sure that dating sites can be great avenues for many people to meet their soul mates, but I do not think that that is where I am going to meet the next person that I need to spend time with. I just had to let the subscription expire and get it out of my system.

My daughters have a much better grasp of what dating is like today than I do, so they are my go to when I need advice. Of course, I am always praying for wisdom from God on the matter as well. But, if I want no nonsense answers to regularly asked dating questions, my girls are the experts. Although I do exercise authority over my children as a parent, we are very much like sisters as well because of all of the darkness that we have had to endure together. Many parents say, "They don't need to know that you're their friend. They need to know you as their parent, their authority." Well, yes I agree with most of that. However, when a family goes through what we've been through, the children need to know that, yes, their mother is the best friend that they will ever have and that they can trust her implicitly. So, yes, I am my daughters' friend because the dynamics of our family are different due to what we've had to endure. They need to know that I am their friend that they can trust so that when I do give them sound advice based on my experience, they know that they can trust me and, therefore, will be more inclined to understand if I tell them that they cannot do something. Anyway, the tables have turned somewhat with my girls according to the dating spectrum. Whenever there is a potential date in the picture, both of my girls get on social media and find out as much about the guy as possible. Yes, they are that protective. I am glad that they want to take care of their Momma like that, though.

One potential pitfall of being a single parent who happens to be widowed is that it is easy to let emotions get the best of you whenever you are lonely. There was one situation where I spent time with this guy, only to find out that he had no intention of dating me. He just wanted to proposition me. Although I did not have sex with him, I allowed myself to get too emotionally connected with him, only to find out that he planned on using me. This did not set too well with me, so I had to put the brakes on that. It's easy to believe that they care when they really do not. I need to stop and explain that I am not a man basher. I am simply explaining my experiences so that other widows, widowers, or those who have lost loved ones will know what to do when they encounter the same kinds of pitfalls that I have experienced. Where I thought I was ready emotionally to get close to a guy, I learned that I really needed to take that step very, very slowly for then on.

Although that was a heart-wrenching experience, it was a lesson to me. God taught me that my standards for what I am looking for need to be realistic, high, not compromising, and firm. Through that experience, I learned what I really want, what I don't want, what I really need, and what I don't need. I need a man who obviously loves God (and not just says that he does-and I can tell the difference!), treats me with respect, reaches out to me by wanting to learn more about my life and personality, is willing to invest in me as a person, wants to know my likes, dislikes, hobbies, will look into my eyes and tell me cares, will not pressure me into physical relations, who generally just wants to be in the same room with me and will be so happy just to breathe the same air that I breathe. He will have to understand that I may not ever want to remarry and it will take me a good while to even share a space with him (hug or kiss) for fear of falling in love. I know that if I feel comfortable enough to allow a guy anywhere close to my lips, I fall for him. That says a lot about the guy because I'm a tough nut to crack when it comes to commitment in dating. It's like that movie Pretty Woman and I quote, "You kissed him on the lips? Did I not teach you anything?!" If I allow him to kiss me on the lips, it's pretty much a done deal. I've fallen.

I know that all of that sounds really selfish, but it is what I want and I think it's out there. What is dangerous, though, is when widows and widowers like me make the mistake of comparing everyone that we are dating to the mate that we had. I had and have to (daily) realize that God might bring someone into my life who is like Roland or he might be totally different and that's okay. I just have to have a handle on my standards and stick with them.

As I step into this dating world post-Roland, I realize the perils therein. As a single woman and mother, I have to be vigilant in making sure that we are not taken advantage of, stolen from, or hurt emotionally. For that reason, I feel that I have to put up this wall of mistrust in my quest to protect the three of us. It is very difficult to know when and if I will be able to let the wall down. I realized that I am afraid; afraid of being hurt emotionally if I allow myself to fall, afraid of being deliberately left to fend for myself again; afraid that the one that I love will die. It is so easy to read all kinds of evil into situations that otherwise would have been meant to be genuine and then I wind up pushing those who want to get close to me far away. I mean, I thought that I knew my husband. Apparently, I did not. I also realized that, where I was in the process of grieving for my husband when I met the first guy, the second guy that I dated could have really been a keeper. Naturally, I fell for him and it tore my heart out because maybe I wasn't quite ready for that emotionally. I wasn't ready to answer questions about the two of us. I thought that I was. He leaned in and so I did, too. He also got scared and bolted, but only after I allowed myself to fall-disaster waiting to happen! It devastated me because I really liked him. This was the first guy that I had dated post-Roland that I didn't compare to my husband in every nitpicky way because this guy was unique all on his own. I haven't heard back from him until today through text and I am sitting here contemplating exactly what I am going to say to him when he calls.

Fast forward to the next day. He did not call. Needless to say, I am feeling like a stupid, gullible little girl because I actually believed everything that he said. I am left with all of these questions. What did I do? Was I not good enough for him? Was I too demanding in my quest to express to him what I really wanted in a man? Did he bolt because there was something wrong with me or was it him? Was he scared and not ready for a Christian relationship even though he professed to be a Christian? Did he feel like he would not be able to step up and truly be the man that I had described that I wanted; a man who loved God more than he loved me so that I would know that he would treat me the way that I needed to be treated? In the wake of all of this happening, I began to hear Satan whispering, "You couldn't even keep your husband. What makes you think that you can hang on to this one!" This made me doubt myself even more. I wondered if I even had "the stuff" to be able to be perceived as impressive or attractive to anyone of the opposite sex again. Everyone was trying to tell me that I was gorgeous inside and out, but I didn't believe it. I had truly lost my touch...Another feeling that I was experiencing was flat out anger. I was angry with both of these men who I fell in love with who had acted as such cowards. What was so hard that Roland had to choose to leave me on this earth in a lurch with nobody to take care of me? Also, what cowardice it takes to just walk away from a budding relationship when you don't think that you can step up and potentially turn away from things in your personal life that are distracting you from being in the will of God; all of this because you are afraid to let someone into your personal world because you were really hurt in your last marriage or because you are afraid to take a risk and reveal more about yourself!

Well, in the waiting and quiet, God has begun to teach me a lot about how I could handle this type of situation should there ever be a next time with another guy. First, I will not answer telephone calls or texts between the hours of 9:00 p.m and 9:00 a.m. unless they are sent by family members. I think that in allowing that, I inadvertently set myself up to look like I was too available and it also compromised my ability to be perceived as a real, Christian lady. God also prompted me to take a break from all social media (dating sites, Facebook, private messenger) for the time being. He helped me understand that it put invisible chains on my life where I felt like I just had to check it regularly. (I no longer felt compelled to message him desperate for a reply which I had done in the previous weeks. This was so wrong of me in the first place! I knew my heart was in such overdrive for attention at this point that I thought that if I purposely disconnected myself from all contact with this guy, I would not make any more stupid mistakes). In trying to contact him constantly, I know that I probably made myself look very weak, vulnerable and desperate for a man. Never again! I will tell you that since I have distanced myself from those things, I feel like a weight has been lifted off of my shoulders and I can breathe. I really don't miss it. You are probably asking, "Well, what if a man tries to reach you and cannot?" I truly believe that if a man really wants to reach me, he will go to great lengths to pursue me and that, no matter what I throw at him, he will not be scared away if he is the strong, Christian man that God has for me. I am not bashing forms of social meeting, per se. I am just saying that it was the best thing for me at the time.

The third thing that God prompted me to do was to just dive into the scriptures head first and spend more time with him. I think that He wants me to get myself well first. This whole dating thing really caused a well of sadness to erupt in me. I don't think that I had truly grieved Roland yet, or maybe, I was just going through another stage of the grieving process because it hurt my heart to the core and I cried rivers. I told me sister, "It seems like your body would run out of water eventually, but my eyes keep making more!" God helped me understand that I was not whole and that I needed to reach out to a support group in order to help myself get well. I knew that I couldn't afford a licensed counselor, so I decided to begin attending meetings at my church once a week where people attend who are going through all types of addictions, grief, strongholds, or anything else that could be considered emotionally debilitating. I feel like, through attending these meetings, maybe I can become more of a whole person so that I can truly experience God's love on another level, do right by my girls and be the balanced mom that they need, and, hopefully, put myself in a position where, if God brings someone special into my life one day, I will be ready to love them with the Christian, Proverbs 31 type of love that he deserves. Finally, God impressed upon me that if a guy takes an interest in me that I was not to even consider spending an ounce of time with him unless that I was convinced that he was regularly plugged into a church actively, attending regularly, and had a strong, evident relationship with Christ. I will tell you ahead of time, the first love after your spouse dies is really difficult, so brace yourself!

My preacher did a dating series lately where he said, "I don't know why people go searching everywhere for the love that they are looking for. They don't have to go looking. It will come to them." God told me just that. He said for me to just sit still, enjoying the quietness and serenity of his love right now, and not reach out to anyone or anywhere for potential dating partners. God is to be my dating guru from now on, and, when he thinks that I am ready, he will bring that person into my path. While I am waiting for God to bring that person to me, I am trying to make sure that I am close to him. I know that

I need to be the best me I can be and be as close to God as possible for me to be mentally and emotionally ready to meet someone new. He's obviously going to have to be a treasure or a needle in a haystack. Either way, it will be fun when it finally does happen.

Journal Entry #10 Hannah's Story

· · ·

HANNAH'S STORY

This is the story of one of my students. She really wanted to include it in the book. This is a classic example of how deeply one can impact others just by the way that he or she chooses to conduct their everyday lives. I never knew that she even saw something different in me until she told me all of this one day when we were talking. It is a little sobering when you think of all of the things that I have been through since she wrote this and she had to see me work through it with God's help. I can only hope that I handled it well considering some of those instances were experiences that I had not been through yet as a widow. Needless to say, I crashed and burned a lot and she watched as God broke me down, but then built me back up again because I knew that I had to depend on him solely to get me through it all. So, this is her story.

One day I went to sign up for GED classes. I was at this one place where nothing was getting done, so I decided after words of encouragement from several people. I started taking classes through the college and that's where I met Ms. Angie Kauffman. When I first met her I did not know what God had in store for me. All I knew is that I had this beautiful, smart, and strong woman for my teacher. She's the kind of teacher that pushes you to be better; be a better version of yourself. She will go out of her way to make sure you understood something even if she had to learn it for herself before teaching you. Well, one day it was just her and I in the classroom. That day, God opened a door that I willingly went through without a second thought and I'm glad I did. You see, what you have to understand about me is that I am very hesitant about who I let into my life and who I tell certain things.

I learned so much about this woman as she did me. She's been through so much. As we talked, I learned about the passing of her husband. If you heard the way that she talked about him, you'd know that was true love; one that everybody wants. Every time she talks about him, you can see the pain in her eyes. I know that she misses him so much. With all of the pain that she has, you would think,

"How in the world does this woman do it!" Well, I'll tell you. God. He has been keeping her afloat this whole time. You would be amazed at how much she loves God. I believe with everything that she has been through, it's actually brought her closer to God. He has molded her into the person she is today. She isn't just a Sunday Christian. She is an everyday devoted Christian. The way she loves our Lord and Savior will make you want to love him just as much. She will make you remember what your knees are for. That's exactly what happened with me, you see. She taught me that with everything that God has allowed to happen to her, she still loves him no less than she did before. That right there stopped me dead in my tracks because two years before I met this woman, with everything in my life that had happened and my best friend dying in a freak car accident, I had been very mad at God. I allowed myself to grow very distant from him. With her help, I am no longer mad with God and the things that he allows to happen in my life. I am more appreciative now. I have a long way to go before I even consider myself to be as close to GED as she is.

You know, I think the most beautiful people in this world are the ones who went through the toughest situations in life, but still somehow manage to keep a smile on their face. Even if she's having a tough day, she will make sure you are okay before even thinking about talking about herself. When she does talk about what is going on in her life, which is not very often, she does it in such a way where it's almost like she belittles herself. If only she saw herself through her daughters' eyes. If only I could get this broken soul to see herself the way that I see her. She is by far the most beautiful broken soul that I have ever met. I believe that is why God put us in one another's lives; to help each other. To love one another. To be something in that we don't have in our lives, but that we really need. She told me that other day that she believed that she needed me more than I needed her. That is far from the truth. We need each other the same amount in order to balance each other out. I honestly cannot imagine what my life would be right now if I had not walked through that door that God had opened. I would probably still be mad at God. I would still be doing all of the things I should have no business doing. I wouldn't have been able to earn my GED. I wouldn't have been able to have met her daughters. When they hurt, I hurt.

I wish that I would have met her before her husband passed away. If you were to ask me if I believed that a part of a person dies when their loved one passes, my answer be yes for her. Nobody is ever the same once somebody that they love dies. It's like it takes a part of us with them. I can guarantee that my teacher was a completely different person when her husband was still alive. I know that I was before my best friend died. Both of us lost a piece of ourselves the day that her husband committed suicide and the say that my best friend was killed in a car accident. We both lost someone very dear to us individually, but found a way to cope with it differently.

It is pretty amazing how someone who loves God just has an aura about them. Miss Angie just has this light in her when the usual person who has gone through similar tragedies would be very dark and moody. She and her girls are so bubbly. She passes the joy that God has replaced her ashes for on to her daughters, which tells me that she loves them unconditionally. Needless to say, I have been very blessed to have this woman in my life that I know that I can go to with any problem and not get judged for it. She will give me the very best advice that she can. I look to her as a mom. I thank God for allowing this wonderful woman to guide me closer to him. I also thank god for giving me somebody to love me and show me the kind of love that I never thought that I deserved. God, I love you very much. Miss Angie, Tori, and Emily, thank you for giving me love and accepting me, listening to my rants, and being willing to pick up the phone and talk to me at any hour that I would call and need you. I just pray that you three know how much you mean to me. I will more than happy to answer the phone at any time that you guys call, good or bad news. I love you with all of my heart and then some. "For I consider that the sufferings of this present time are not worth comparing with the glory that is going to be revealed to us." Romans 8:18 NLT.

It's me again-Angie…I know that people have to go through all sorts of situations when their loved ones die or even when they have other figurative "deaths" in their lives like divorce or when a loved one just all of sudden decides to leave them for no logical reason at all. It hurts and I understand. I sincerely hope that this book has helped in some way to soothe any hurts that you have had to deal with. I hope that it has offered some perspective in times of clear uncertainty. I do not have all of the answers, but I do know that when I don't know which direction to go in that praying is always the right answer. God is unchanging and will never flake out on you like mere humans will. He is the greatest romance that a person will ever have because he will never, ever let you down. If given the choice of being one of those people who has never had any huge tragedies in their lives or one who has had to crawl through the rubble of despair, I would much rather be one who went through tough circumstances. I believe that we who have had to deal with extreme sadness possess the ability to be real to others and are better equipped to minister to others who are going through crushing times. God does not allow us to go through tough times in order to hurt us. He apparently sees hidden potential strength that he wants to bring out in us. It is up to us to step up to the plate and allow him to help us improve ourselves in the process and take us into a much deeper walk with him. After all, when it's all said and done, it is going to be just you and him in eternity if you truly have accepted him into your heart. Why not dive in and cherish the most wonderful relationship that you could ever have both in this temporary life on Earth and eternally? It's okay to be broken. We do leak because we have cracks, but God has to fill those places in order for us to be whole again.

About the Author

Angie Kauffman is an instructor for Adult Education at South Georgia Technical College in Americus, Georgia. She has been a teacher by day for over 20 years, a writer by night. She is a very busy single mom to two beautiful young ladies and is active in her church as a worship leader. God's insight through a tragic life experience has led her to want to be transparent and share with others about how God is helping her muddle through even though she has often felt broken and unable to be used.

Printed in the United States
By Bookmasters

bitterness we may have in our hearts and put love and compassion in its place.

We Can't Change the Past

There is not one thing we can do to change what has already happened, so put it there, in the past, and forget about it. If we don't let go of the past, we actually tie the sin of the person who hurt us to ourselves, and that includes all the curses and consequences that go along with it. That makes the devil do a happy dance, because he has got us in his kingdom. The hurt we feel as we are growing up can continue to hurt us as we grow older. There are people who live in pain as adults because of even one time that they were hurt badly by someone when they were a child. That kind of pain will manifest itself in our thoughts, in our self-images, in our relationships with others, and in our relationship with God. It comes out through bad dreams and in our emotions, which will gradually make us very sick. If we look to someone else to give us the love we desire, it is like an act of idolatry. It turns into a relationship where we want a lot from them and they really don't have anything to give back. The other person can never satisfy us, so it makes us feel even worse. We become pushy, and people want to get away from us, and that makes us feel more rejected and unloved.

God the Father is our source of all love, caring, nurturing, and protection.

God the Word is our source of worthiness and forgiveness (Colossians 1:14; 2:10).

God, the Holy Spirit is our source of power (Acts 1:8).

God is love and any spirit that separates us from God's love is an "antichrist spirit" (1 John 4:18; John 3:16).

We were created in God's image, so we *are* love. Let's get rid of all those lies from Satan and accept who we are and let God change us. If we do not love ourselves, it is like saying to our Creator, "You didn't do a good job when you created me!" When we do that, we are putting our thoughts higher than God's thoughts. He is our Sovereign Creator. He made us, and He said we are "very good", so we must believe that we are very good, because God said so (Ephesians 1 and 2).

In order to be *free,* we have to leave all people from the past behind and find out who we are in Christ. When we are hurt, it's not really about us; it's the person acting out against us and treating us badly who is to blame. That person has an evil spirit manifesting though them. But if we are not sure of who God says we are, we might think it is all about us and allow this sin into our lives. We were created in God's image, so we are love. Let's get rid of all those lies from Satan. Let's accept who we are in Christ and let God change us. After all, He is our Sovereign

Creator. Unloving spirits will not go without a fight! You will need to continually watch out for signs of their interference and boot them out (Hebrews 4:11). We have been made worthy by our Heavenly Father to walk in Christ's freedom (Colossians 1:12–14).

*Self-pity is also a factor
of the unloving spirit.*

Unloving Kingdom

The "unloving kingdom" is all about *self.* The enemy will use all kinds of situations in our lives to try to steal us away from God. Traumas, broken hearts, and difficult times are open doors for the *spirit of self-pity* to take advantage of us, because we are at a vulnerable point in our lives. When we've been wounded and are down in spirit, the spirit of self-pity will come and falsely shield us from additional pain. If we were hurt when we were growing up, the spirit of self-pity will tell us we can't trust anyone to help us. We may think we have to do it on our own, because we can't trust anyone. The spirit of self-pity will pretend to comfort us and will chain us to past hurts and events. This doesn't help but only keeps us anxious and worrying about our problems and circumstances. This spirit tries to block our minds so we are not thinking clearly. Self-pity is also addictive, because it tells us that we don't need to take care of things in our lives. Similar to alcohol or drugs, it numbs our feelings to what is really going on. Self-pity doesn't help us, it hinders us. It acts as if it is comfort, but it is actually taking our focus off what is really happening around us. There is a choice! We can choose to face up to what we have to deal with, and we can choose to change our circumstances. Self-pity will keep us from taking action or control of our lives. God is always there to help us; we *can* overcome self-pity. The Holy Spirit is our comforter and friend, and we can always trust Him. We can always talk to Father God. He enjoys hangin' out with us and hearing our prayers. He will help us face what we have to face, if we only trust in Him.

Blessed be God, even the Father of our Lord Jesus Christ, the Father of mercies, and the God of all comfort; who comforts us in all our tribulation, that we may be able to comfort them which are in any trouble, by the comfort wherewith we ourselves are comforted of God.
♥ 2 Corinthians 1:3–4 NKJV

What shall we then say to these things? If God be for us, who can be against us?
♥ Romans 8:31 NKJV

Our Heavenly Daddy created us, and He loves us with an everlasting, unconditional love, and because He loves us so much, we choose to like ourselves and like who we are. We have to make the choice to love ourselves and be comfortable with who God created us to be. We are ambassadors for Christ, and our goal is to bring the Kingdom of Heaven to earth and come against the enemy. Satan is a liar. *We have the power!* Jesus told us to go forth and spread the gospel, heal the sick, cast out demons, and raise the dead – all in the power of His Holy Name. He also gave us power and authority over all demons and over diseases. He told us we can do even greater things than He did. God loves us! We are His children – His chosen ones.

Who Will You Choose to Serve?

Will you choose God, our Creator and Heavenly Daddy, or Satan, the liar, murderer, and accuser? Choose the route of *victory*, as we renew our minds, change our thought patterns, and stay on Victory Street. This way the devil takes the route of defeat, and we have put him under our feet and stomped on him! *He has no power over us!*

Let's keep believing God and not allow those old lies from the enemy to affect the way we live our lives. The enemy has been teaching us to go his way, and he will try his best to keep us going in the wrong direction of defeat, but we will overcome, as we renew our minds, by practicing what God teaches us in the Bible every day. We *will* stay free in Christ.

We have the victory!

Chapter Four

ROSE OF SHARON

GOD HAS A GLORIOUS DESIGN and plan for our lives. By an act of God's mercy and grace, and by faith, we can be restored to a right relationship with our Heavenly Father. Because of forgiveness, we, as believers, can present our lives, talents, gifts, and abilities, whatever they might be, as an act of worship to God. It is important to realize our position before God. It doesn't matter what we've done, Christ's blood not only redeems our past, but supernaturally changes our future, creating a future that is beautiful and bright. Like the Rose of Sharon, we will blossom in full array and be pleasing to God. Be encouraged, and know that God is in control. Wherever we are in our walk with God, we can do our best each step of the way blossoming where we are planted at each stage of growth, moving on when the next season comes around.

> *And we know that all things work together for good to those who love God, to those who are the called according to His purpose.*
>
> ♥ Romans 8:28 NKJV

We have all been given talents and spiritual gifts. We need to use the giftedness that God has given us in service to Him. Both talents and spiritual gifts are from God. Both grow in effectiveness with use. Both are intended to be used on behalf of others, not ourselves (1 Corinthians12:7). As the two great commandments deal with loving God and others, it follows that we should use our talents for those purposes. But to whom and when talents and spiritual gifts are given differs. A person (regardless of his belief in God or in Christ) is given natural talent as a result of a combination of genetics (e.g. music, art, mathematics) or because God desired to endow certain individuals with certain talents. Spiritual gifts are given to believers by the Holy Spirit when they place their faith in Christ for the forgiveness of their sins (Romans 12:3,6). The Holy Spirit gives new believers spiritual gifts in accordance with God's Divine plan and purpose for them (1 Corinthians 12:11).

We are assured that God, being a partner in our labour, will make all things work together and have a good plan for those who love Him and are called according to His design and purpose. He also comforts us with the knowledge that nothing can separate us from His love. The knowledge of God's grace and forgiveness frees us not only from sin but from anxiety, depression, and a negative self-image. Forgiveness restores our relationship with our Creator, allowing us to find meaning and purpose, and it lifts the heavy weight of guilt and shame. The stress flows out, and the salvation flows in.

When we show love,
it is a powerful act of spiritual warfare
that removes anxiety from the environment.

Scripture Gives Us the Law of Love and Emphasizes the Importance of Love

I know and am convinced by the Lord Jesus that there is nothing unclean of itself; but to him who considers anything to be unclean, to him it is unclean. Yet if your brother is grieved because of your food, you are no longer walking in love. Do not destroy with your food the one for whom Christ died. Therefore do not let your good be spoken of as evil; for the kingdom of God is not eating and drinking, but righteousness and peace and joy in the Holy Spirit. For he who serves Christ in these things is

acceptable to God and approved by men. Therefore let us pursue the things which make for peace and the things by which one may edify another.
♥ Romans 14:14–19 NKJV

If we don't have love, we are nothing. Love is the key to life and a healthy love – life keeps us healthy. Loving kindness is better than life, and we are to love our neighbours as we love ourselves. We must love ourselves first, so we can love others. When we show our love and give our love to others, we blossom like an array of beautiful flowers so that all who see us will know that we have the love of God in us.

Hatred stirs up contentions, but love covers all transgressions.
♥ Proverbs 10:12 AMP

"May he kiss me with the kisses of his mouth!"
[Solomon arrives; she turns to him, saying,]
"For your love is better than wine.
♥ Song of Solomon 1:2 AMP

When Jesus talked to us, He often used fruit to explain His relationship with us. Jesus always kept things simple. Jesus is saying that we cannot do anything without Him. So if He is in us and we are in Him, we can go and bear much fruit. If a person does not dwell in the Lord Jesus Christ, he is discarded like a broken branch. Such branches wither and are thrown into the fire, where they are burned.

Remain in Me, and I [will remain] in you. Just as
no branch can bear fruit by itself without remaining
in the vine, neither can you [bear fruit, producing
evidence of your faith] unless you remain in Me. I
am the Vine; you are the branches. The one who
remains in Me and I in him bears much fruit, for
[otherwise] apart from Me [that is, cut off from vital
union with Me] you can do nothing. If you remain in
Me and My words remain in you [that is, if we are
vitally united and My message lives in your heart],
ask whatever you wish and it will be done for you.

♥ John 15:4–5, 7 AMP

Jesus said, "When you produce much fruit, My Father is honoured and glorified, and you prove yourselves to be true followers of Mine. I have loved you, just as the Father has loved Me; continue in His love with Me (John 15:8-9). We must let our conduct be without covetousness and be content with the things that we have, for our Lord and Saviour, Jesus Christ, said He will never leave us nor forsake us. That is why we can say boldly, "The Lord is our helper. We will not fear. What can man do to us?"

At first glance, it may seem strange or awkward to compare love to vineyards, or buildings such as watchtowers, or animals, lamb's wool, and fruits such as pomegranates. But as we take a closer examination, these analogies reveal the mindset of the ancient lovers. Love's value is measured in function as well as appearance. How is our love's value measured? Could we say the same? True love is giving, unselfish, supportive, honest, and unconditional. Solomon called his beloved the "Rose of Sharon"; by doing so, he brings to mind the symbol of God's blessing which was represented by the blossoming of this flower. In the Song of Solomon, love is depicted in all its beauty and glory. When we read the Song of Solomon, we see that love's greatest attributes are highlighted. Love's deeper qualities are also extolled. There was no lack of words to describe Solomon's praise of the Shulamite woman's beauty. Can we say the same about our love lives with spouses or others? Love never fails. If we have broken relationship or marriages, they did not have love in the first place. The greatest gift is the spirit of love.

Though I speak with the tongues of men and of angels, but have not love, I have become sounding brass or a clanging cymbal. And though I have the gift of prophecy, and understand all mysteries and all knowledge, and though I have all faith, so that I could remove mountains, but have not love, I am nothing. And though I bestow all my goods to feed the poor, and though I give my body to be burned, but have not love, it profits me nothing. Love suffers long and is kind; love does not envy; love does not parade itself, is not puffed up; does not behave rudely, does not seek its own, is not provoked, thinks no evil; does not rejoice in iniquity, but rejoices in the truth; bears all things, believes all things, hopes all things, endures all things. Love never fails. But whether there are prophecies, they will fail; whether there are tongues, they will cease; whether there is knowledge, it will vanish away. For we know in part and we prophesy in part. But when that which is perfect has come, then that which is in part will be done away. When I was a child, I spoke as a child, I understood as a child, I thought as a child; but when I became a man, I put away childish things. For now we see in a mirror dimly, but then face to face. Now I know in part, but then I shall know just as I also am known. And now abide faith, hope, love, these three; but the greatest of these is love.

♥ 1 Corinthians 13:1–13 NKJV

God did not give us a spirit of fear, but of power, love and a sound mind.

♥ 2 Timothy 1:7 NKJV

There is no other commandment greater than love, according to 1 Corinthians 13:13. We must walk in love. 1 Corinthians 14:1 tells us to pursue love, so we must eagerly pursue and seek to acquire this love. We should make it a goal, the greatest quest. We must earnestly desire and cultivate the spiritual endowment gifts, and especially that we may prophesy, interpret the divine will and purpose in inspired preaching and teaching. We must learn to allow God to do the unexpected in our lives and not limit God with locked-in thinking about love. We need to unlock our faith and allow God to touch us, reach us, and come to us in unexpected ways through people, places, and events in our lives. In doing so, we can come alive and, like a rosebud, we will open up and blossom into beautiful specimens of God's amazing love – like the Rose of Sharon!

Stars can't shine without darkness

...... that you may become blameless and harmless, children of God without fault in the midst of a crooked and perverse generation, among whom you shine as lights in the world, holding fast the word of life, so that I may rejoice in the day of Christ that I have not run in vain or labored in vain.

♥ Philippians 2:15-16 NKJV

By doing the unexpected, God can use the insignificant to accomplish the impossible. We can expect miracles! Loving ourselves and others is like a miracle. Jesus says we should love the Lord our God with all our hearts, all our souls, and all our minds (Matthew 22:36–37). Jesus added: "You shall love your neighbour as yourself" (Matthew 22:39). The two commandments are contingent upon each other. Can you see how big and wide love is? Love is life! Jesus lived a life that was worthy of what He teaches us. You see throughout Jesus's ministry that His goal was to reveal the love of God through His love for all people. He taught His disciples – and us – "As the Father loved me, I also have loved you (John 15:9).

A new commandment I give to you, that you love one another; as I have loved you, that you also love one another.

♥ John 13:34 NKJV

The supreme act of love came when Jesus Christ willingly died on the cross to bring us into an intimate relationship with God. Through the cross, Jesus Christ declared His love for all people. Because of His love in our lives, we now can love each other.

The cross is a symbol of that love relationship.

As God loves us, so we should love each other. Our lives are to reflect this relationship, because from the love of God we receive the feeling of self-worth that enables us to love other people without the fear of rejection. We can live lives that say, "I love you" and "God loves you". God is light, and if we walk in the light, as He is in the light, we will have fellowship with one another. The Holy Spirit lives in us and will always guide us and lead us in truth. God is holiness, and we can trust in His love. The reason the Son of God appeared was to destroy the devil's work. If we don't love ourselves and love others, we are doing the devil's work for him. *Don't do it!* Do God's work. It is very profitable and rewarding lifelong.

Jesus also said, "As the Father (God) loves me, I also love you." Loving one another is an example of love. Jesus Christ laid down His life for us. This is how we know God's amazing love for us. We have the love of Christ in us as born-again believers. Jesus also went on to say:

> *But whoever has this world's goods, and sees his brother in need, and shuts up his heart from him, how does the love of God abide in him?*
> ♥ 1 John 3:17 NKJV

Spirit of Love

We are to not only love in word and in tongue (by our words) but in deed and in truth, as well. God gave us the "spirit of love" (2 Timothy 1:7). We can choose to love, or we can choose not to love. If we choose not to love, we will be walking in disobedience. According to Scripture, when we walk in disobedience, curses such as sickness and disease will come upon us. These curses are of the devil. We will wither and die like a flower that receives no water or sunshine. When we choose to love, we will be walking in obedience. Blessings will come upon us and overtake us when we obey the voice of the Lord, and we will blossom like the Rose of Sharon with the sweet fragrance of God's love (Deuteronomy 28:1–14). God gave us the message of love, hope, and forgiveness for all mankind. It is an awesome feeling when we have love in our hearts and we can walk in that love.

Therefore be imitators of God [copy Him and follow His example], as well–beloved children [imitate their father]. And walk in love, [esteeming and delighting in one another] as Christ loved us and gave Himself up for us, a slain offering and sacrifice to God [for you, so that it became] a sweet fragrance. But immorality (sexual vice) and all impurity [of lustful, rich, wasteful living] or greediness must not even be named among you, as is fitting and proper among saints (God's consecrated people). Let there be no filthiness (obscenity, indecency) nor foolish and sinful (silly and corrupt) talk, nor coarse jesting, which are not fitting or becoming; but instead voice your thankfulness [to God]. For be sure of this: that no person practicing sexual vice or impurity in thought or in life, or one who is covetous [who has lustful desire for the property of others and is greedy for gain] – for he [in effect] is an idolater – has any inheritance in the kingdom of Christ and of God. Let no one delude and deceive you with empty excuses and groundless arguments [for these sins], for through these things the wrath of God comes upon the sons of rebellion and disobedience. So do not associate or be sharers with them.

♥ Ephesians 5:1–7 AMP

Clearly we can see that living a Godly lifestyle is very important, not only to God but to us. We cannot be immoral persons and have good lives. We open up ourselves to sickness, disease, broken relationships, etc., and that is not the way God created us to live. That's why these Scriptures are so important. They tell us how to walk in love.

> *Look carefully then how you walk! Live purposefully and worthily and accurately, not as the unwise and witless, but as wise (sensible, intelligent people), making the very most of the time [buying up each opportunity], because the days are evil.*
>
> ♥ Ephesians 5:15–16 AMP

When we put these Scriptures into practice, and with wisdom, understanding, and discernment, we will walk in wholeness. I am not suggesting being a doormat for anyone. The Bible says to be as wise as a serpent and as harmless as a dove.

> *I therefore, the prisoner for the Lord, appeal to and beg you to walk (lead a life) worthy of the [divine] calling to which you have been called [with behaviour that is a credit to the summons to God's service, living as becomes you] with complete lowliness of mind (humility) and meekness (unselfishness, gentleness, mildness), with patience, bearing with one another and making allowances because you love one another. Be eager and strive earnestly to guard and keep the harmony*

and oneness of [and produced by] the Spirit in the binding power of peace. There is one body and one Spirit – just as there is also one hope [that belongs] to the calling you received – There is one Lord, one faith, one baptism, One God and Father of [us] all, Who is above all [Sovereign over all], pervading all and [living] in [us] all.

♥ Ephesians 4:1–6 AMP

Unity is also a big part of walking in love. Where there is unity, there is strength and harmony among the children of God. Believers are beautiful, clothed in the righteousness of Christ, and fragrant with the scent of his Spirit. Like the Rose of Sharon, believers blossom and thrive in the "Son" light of righteousness.

Love is like the Rose of Sharon;
it requires cultivating,
feeding and watering.
Without these, love, like the flower,
withers and dies.

Chapter Five

KEYS TO FREEDOM

FREEDOM IS NOT JUST THE act of casting off one's chains but living in a way that respects God and loves others. The walk to freedom may not be easy, and many of us will have to pass through the valley of the shadow of death again and again before we reach the mountaintop. In order to get free, there are some biblical principles that we need to apply to our lives.

The Major Key

Forgiveness is a major key to freedom. Forgiveness goes hand in hand with love. In order to truly love, we have to walk in forgiveness, to always be ready to forgive the other person. Our Lord Jesus Christ forgave everyone who came to Him and asked for forgiveness. He is always ready to forgive us, because He loves us so much. We are to have that same heart.

> *But there is forgiveness with You [just what man needs], that You may be reverently feared and worshiped.*
>
> ♥ Psalm 130:4 AMP

There is forgiveness with Him, that He may be reverenced, loved, and honoured. We are made in God's image, so we should have that same forgiveness. To understand forgiveness, we have to deal with its root cause, which is bitterness. Bitterness can start with an offence. For example, if someone says something to upset us or hurt us, we may be offended and perhaps become angry. Those spoken words were an offence to our hearts. When we take offence, we bring on bitterness and unforgiveness. This is an open door for the spirits of resentment, retaliation, anger, hatred, violence, domestic violence, and murder, including murder with the tongue. Now the *principality of bitterness* has its foot in the door, and the goal is to defile and destroy us and those around us (Hebrews 12:15).

Forgiveness is not for the other person.
It is for you!
It is the responsibility of the other person
to deal with their own unforgiveness.

Joanie: Unforgiveness, Bitterness, and Anger

When I went to visit Joan in her home, she was full of anger and bitterness, which was directed towards her mother and her ex-husband. She was so angry towards her ex-husband that it reflected in the way she treated her present husband, who loved her very much and was caring for her because she was wheelchair bound. The Holy Spirit spoke to me and told me that the reason Joan was confined to a wheelchair was because of the unforgiveness that she had towards these two people. I was able to speak into her heart and show her how she could forgive her mom and ex-husband. I explained to her that forgiveness was not for the other person but for her own freedom. When people hold on to unforgiveness, they are in bondage to the past and the people who hurt them. When they forgive someone, it sets them free to live their lives and put the people who hurt them in God's hands for Him to judge. My wife stood in proxy for Joan's mom and spoke words of healing into her heart, and Joan was able to forgive her mom. Next, I stood in proxy for her ex-husband, and she was able to forgive him. We dealt with spirits of bitterness and anger, and Joan's whole countenance began to change. She looked brighter and lighter, and she seems to have peace. I prayed over her and told her to get up and walk. She was able to get up and walk a few steps while holding on to furniture. When we left her house, she was smiling and happy and proud of being able to walk. We trust the Lord for continued healing in her body.

The practice of forgiveness is the most important contribution to healing. Those who are free of resentful thoughts will find peace.

Be on the alert and look after one another, to see that no root of resentment, anger, bitterness, or hatred takes hold and causes trouble and torment. Many people become contaminated and defiled by these, and we want to make sure we continue in God's grace of unmerited favour and spiritual blessing (Hebrews 12:15). Scripture tells us that if people choose not to forgive, they can become sick with disease and even disabled. I have seen evidence of this in the lives of people I have counselled.

We must have a forgiving heart and the ability to discern the spirits. Our forgiveness has to be genuine and sincere. Jesus has that forgiving heart. He forgives everyone who comes to Him and asks for forgiveness. If you make a mistake and mess up, He will forgive you. Our goal is to have the same mind as Jesus. We are seated with Jesus Christ, and we are to look down from heaven. Earth is supposed to be a reflection of heaven, and we, as Christians, must reflect heaven on earth. This is what our Lord Jesus Christ instructed us to do. We should meditate on the goodness of God. We must renew our minds daily by reading the Word of God.

> *Brethren, whatever things are true, whatever things are noble, whatever things are just, whatever things are pure, whatever things are lovely, whatever things are of good report, and if there is anything praiseworthy, meditate on these things.*
> ♥ Philippians 4:8 NKJV

We can filter out the negative doctrines which taught judgment and legalism, and we can replace them with the gospel of hope, love, peace, patience, kindness, forgiveness, and gentleness, against which there is no law. Jesus is the fulfilment of the law, and Jesus is the freedom to which the law points.

Immune System

Let's take a look at something that is very important to humans and our immune systems. The spiritual enemy (Satan) wants to destroy our immune systems, which are centred in the marrow of our bones. Our blood has its origin in the marrow, where it is manufactured. The T–cells, macrophages, killer cells, and white and red corpuscles are found in the marrow (Wright, 2009). Here are some ways that Satan tries to access our marrow or immune system:

- controlling our thoughts
- trying to make his evil spirituality our spirituality
- trying to get us to follow his law of sin
- trying to break up relationships
- stirring up strife and promoting conflict
- promoting inappropriate reactions
- initiating verbal, physical, emotional, and sexual abuse
- speaking to us in the first person as though his thoughts were our own

It is the Spirit Who gives life [He is the Life–giver]; the flesh conveys no benefit whatever [there is no profit in it]. The words (truths) that I have been speaking to you are spirit and life.
♥ John 6:63 AMP

Jesus said that the words that He speaks to us are spirit, and they are life. That is why it is so important to walk in forgiveness.

Choose life!

Thoughts

When thoughts come into our minds, discern from where they are coming. If they are positive or good thoughts, they are from God; if they are negative or evil thoughts, they are from Satan.

Ask yourself,

 "Who told me that?"

Only good and perfect gifts come from our Heavenly Father, who never changes (James 1:17). Our thoughts have a lot to do with how we love. Don't be fooled by the devil. God's grace is released through His love and mercy and expressed in the act of forgiving each other. It is very easy to let our guard down. The following Scripture gives us an example of how thoughts can enter our minds:

> *He said to them, "But who do you say that I am?" Simon Peter answered and said, "You are the Christ, the Son of the living God." Jesus answered and said to him, "Blessed are you, Simon Bar–Jonah, for flesh and blood has not revealed this to you, but My Father who is in heaven."*
>
> ♥ Matthew 16:15–17 NKJV

Here, Peter confesses that Jesus is the Christ, the Son of the living God. Jesus said that it was His Father in heaven who had revealed this understanding to Peter. The Father would have done this by His Holy Spirit, speaking into Peter's spirit, through beta brain-wave activity to Peter's brain, where the thought occurred.

When Jesus told His disciples that He must go to Jerusalem and suffer many things from the elders, chief priests, and scribes, and be killed and be raised the third day, Peter took Him aside and began to rebuke Him, saying, "Far be it from You, Lord; this shall not happen to You!" But Jesus turned and said to Peter, "Get behind Me, Satan! You are an offence to Me, for you are not mindful of the things of God but the things of men" (Matthew 16:22–23).

In this instance, it was Satan speaking through Peter, using the same pathway of thought, through beta brain-wave activity, to Peter's brain. Note that Jesus rebuked Satan, not Peter.

According to studies by Dr Caroline Leaf, every time you have a thought, it actively changes your brain and your body, for better or worse. Toxic thoughts as a result of an especially horrific trauma don't just creep into our minds. Toxic thoughts affect people in all stages of life, in every part of the world, every day. Even something small, like comments made by others, can become toxic if we dwell on them. These thoughts need to be dealt with or swept away. If we continue to focus on toxic thoughts, they will grow and become larger and more difficult to overcome.

Whatever you think about the most grows,
so build healthy trees in your minds
if you want a healthy reality!
♥ Dr Caroline Leaf

Dr Leaf describes it this way: "Like an expert chef, we can choose to put only tasty thoughts and feelings into our cells. Putting toxic thoughts into our brains is like putting poison in our food. That is why God tells us to control our thought life; putting healthy thoughts into our minds is akin to that dash of fresh basil on top of the lasagne." With the thoughts we choose, we can either poison or strengthen our immune systems, bodies and minds, which will, whether we want it or not, have an impact on our bodily health and our spiritual development!

Meditate on good things (Philippians 4:8), not on toxic, poisonous things. Dr Leaf's research proves that healthy thoughts increase the gamma waves in our brains, which means we increase our attention, memory, and learning capacities. Her research has shown that with healthy thinking we build up portions of our brains that produce happiness. Science also shows that meditating on good things, like what the Bible teaches, improves moods in a way far superior way to antidepressants! When it comes to aging, research has shown that older people with healthy attitudes live seven and a half years longer! The thoughts we put into our brains have powerful genetic effects on the production of healing proteins in our bodies.

What we think, feel, and believe constantly changes the genetic expression and chemical composition of our bodies on a moment–by–moment basis. High stress levels, which are the result of poisonous, toxic thoughts, suck biochemical resources away from cell repair and kill brain cells.

When we understand that every feeling and thought we have changes our brains and our bodies, we can actually take some control over our mental and physical health, which will make a huge difference to our lives and the lives of those around us. *Wow!* When we bring our thoughts into captivity to Christ Jesus and choose life, we can consciously change our emotions, thoughts, and prayers to be positive.

Ask yourself,

 "Who told me that?"

Things that happen in life are usually beyond our control, but we do have control over our reactions (which are thoughts) to these situations. We have the ability to *choose* our thoughts and focus on thoughts that are good, which will lead to healthier life. Toxic thinking will target our emotions, words, choices, dreams, faith, touch, seriousness, schedules, love, and our health. The result of toxic thinking is stress in our bodies, and this type of stress is far more than just a fleeting emotion. *Stress* is a term used to explain strain on the body's systems as a result of toxic thinking. It harms the body and the mind, causing issues from patchy memory to mental health problems as well as immune system, heart, and digestive problems.

Dr Leaf points out that no system of the body is spared when stress is running rampant. A massive body of research collectively shows that up to 80 per cent of physical, emotional, and mental health issues today could be a direct result of our thought lives. But there is hope! We can break the cycle and start building healthy patterns to bring peace to our stormy thought lives.

Thinking God's thoughts activates
His love and strength in us.

I can do all things through Christ who strengthens me.
♥ Philippians 4:13 NKJV

We have the answer – Jesus Christ.

Design of Hope

We are not victims of biology. God has given us a design of hope. We can renew our minds, change, and heal. Science really does prove that thoughts can be measured, that they affect every area of our lives, and best of all, that the brain really can change.

There are only two types of emotions, each with their own anatomy and physiology. These are love and fear. All other emotions are variations of these. Out of love come emotions of joy, trust, caring, peace, contentment, patience, kindness, gentleness, etc. Fear-based emotions include bitterness, anger, hatred, rage, anxiety, guilt, shame, inadequacy, depression, confusion, etc. These emotions directly affect our bodies; the amount of chemicals released is based on which group the emotions belong to, either the love-based or fear-based group.

When we experience love emotions, our brains and bodies function differently – better, actually, than if we experience fear emotions. The negative fear-based emotions force the body into backup systems just to hold the fear in check, which is not ideal and not the first choice. Science and the Bible teach us not to fear but to love. Our feelings are the emotions attached to our thoughts. A peaceful feeling reflects healthy thoughts. Toxic thoughts trigger negative and anxious emotions, which produce biochemicals that cause stress in the body. These are stored in your mind as well as in the cells in your body. Healthy, non-toxic thoughts help nurture and create a positive foundation in the neural networks of the mind. These positive thoughts strengthen positive reaction chains and release biochemicals, such as endorphins and serotonin, from the brain's natural pharmacy. Bathed in these positive environments, intellect flourishes, and with it mental and physical health. Fix your thoughts on what is true, and honourable, and right, and pure, and lovely, and admirable. Think about those things that are excellent and trustworthy of praise (Philippians 4:8).

Change your thoughts and you change your world.
♥ Norman Vincent Peale

When people don't accept God's promises and tragedy strikes, they wonder why God allowed it to happen. It happened because they did not appropriate the promises of God. They did not believe or think the promises were for them. They may even have believed that they were for someone else. I have experienced this in my life. All we have to do is act on God's Word and believe for these things to come to pass in our lives.

We have to learn to listen to the voice of God. I believe that if we could look back into events and situations, we would find that every time a person had a catastrophe, God's Holy Spirit had either tried to warn them beforehand or there was an angel that intervened. I have had an angel pull me back from getting hit by a truck, and an angel helped me on the side of a highway when my car broke down in the middle of nowhere in Canada. These experiences let you know that what God says in His Word is true. Ministering angels are servants of God, and their duty is to work for us, minister to us, and help us fight the battles. The angels hearken to the voice of God's Word (Psalm 103:20).

Entry Points or Open Doors

There are events in our lives that are open doors for the enemy kingdom to come into our lives and set up a stronghold. An example of such a life event might be the passing away of a loved one. Some people just can't let go, and this can bring in a "spirit of depression". There are people who are always afraid; no matter what, they always walk in fear. Something serious happens in their lives that opens a door for the spirit of fear to take up a stronghold. Sometimes, if we were hurt badly when we were little, we may walk around feeling sad all the time. This is a "spirit of heaviness" that we can't seem to shake. A car accident can cause trauma and opens a door for the spirit of fear. We think the event is going to happen again and again. Fear is projecting into the future what might happen. Most things we fear never happen!

Pearl: Spirit of Fear

Pearl came to see me with many problems. One of them was fear after a close encounter with another car. It wasn't even an accident, but the trauma from the close call cause her to be afraid to drive again. She had to have someone bring her to the appointment with me. After breaking off trauma and dealing with the spirit of fear, Pearl was able to drive to her next session on her own and even gave us a lift to the store on her way home.

Satan is against God! If God wants us in His Kingdom, Satan will do what he can to draw us away from God. If Satan had his way in our lives, we would already be dead. So, when you think about it, we have already overcome at this level!

When we look back at the past, we can see what God has done for us and how He has kept us alive, even though we have made some poor choices and have sinned. We can also see where Satan has come into our lives even through our ancestors, so we know what to work on to kick the enemy out of our lives. Sin, and the curses that are consequences of sin, can be passed down through the generations and can play havoc in our lives. We have to identify these curses, because they could be the root issues behind sickness and disease. When we identify the root issue (i.e., unforgiveness, bitterness, etc.) and deal with it, the healing will come. We should always be thinking about who we need to forgive. Always begin with forgiveness, and always walk in forgiveness. Forget by choosing not to dwell on that which is forgiven and in the past. We have no right to keep in front of us what God has put behind Him.

Keys to Freedom

We block out experiences that have hurt us so they can't hurt us anymore. The enemy keeps reminding us of the event. The enemy doesn't want us to forget. He wants to keep torturing us with the pain of the event. If we recognize this, we can deal with it. If there are blocks in our memories, we can ask the Holy Spirit to show us how we reacted when the event happened. We can take that reaction to the Lord and "repent" for any way that we agreed with the enemy kingdom and were bitter and afraid. God will free us of what is going on inside.

When we react or take offence to something or someone that hurt us, we open the door for the "curse" to come into our lives. If someone hits us, the enemy wants us to hit them back! Scripture tells us that if we see our enemy hungry, we should buy him food, or if he's thirsty, we should give him a drink. In doing this, we will surprise him with goodness. We can't let evil get the best of us! Rather, get the best of evil, by doing good (Romans 12:21). We can love the enemy. It works, it's fun, and we gain the freedom! We don't receive the offence. When they yell at us, we smile back at them! They don't know what to do. When someone hurts us, they are the ones who have sinned before God. It is their responsibility, not ours!

Satan Is a Thief

God knows us and knows how He wants us to respond. He only has love, hope, peace, and joy for us. There is one word for the law of God, and that is "love". The enemy wants to steal God's love from us. One of the ways he does this is by getting us to agree to retaliation instead of love. We must put value on people. The enemy is very sneaky. He tricks us into not loving the person. When we can't love someone, it causes torment in our bodies, souls, and spirits, and it actually hurts us. God loves us so much that he wants us to have love in all our relationships. That doesn't mean that we go back for more to the person who hurt us. *No!* But we need to keep love in our hearts, so we can receive love from God and others. That way, we can also stop blaming ourselves. The blame belongs to the enemy.

> *You shall love the Lord your God with all your heart, all your soul, all your strength, and all your mind. Also, love your neighbour the same as you love yourself.*
>
> ♥ Luke 10:27 NKJV

When we take an offence, Romans 12:21 tells us not to let ourselves be overcome by evil but to overcome, or master, evil with good. What the offenders did is sin before God. It is their responsibility. How we respond is our responsibility. This is obedience to God. A proper reaction protects us from the curse. We need to forgive others, repent for any response that does not line up with the Word of God, and always walk in forgiveness.

Six Steps to Freedom

1. *Recognize* how the enemy tricked us and how we agreed when we were hurt.

2. *Be responsible* for this and admit to it.

3. *Repent.*

4. *Renounce.*

5. *Remove* it from our lives.

6. *Resist* the temptation, and don't go back to it. Be filled with our Heavenly Father's love.

Entry points, or open doors, are things in our lives that allow the enemy to come into our spirits, souls, and bodies.

Examples of Entry Points

- *Curses* that have come down to us through our generations are open doors or entry points. Curses are reinforced through the spirit of fear. There are curses that seem to be the same from generation to generation. These are called "familiar spirits". We've all heard of alcohol running in families. Crime, molestation, and abuse are also familiar spirits that come down through family lines. These curses can also be passed down from clubs or groups that our parents or grandparents belonged to, such as the Lodge, or Freemasonry. We can be set free!

- The *baby in the womb* can hear what we say! We have to be careful of what we say when we are around someone who is expecting a baby. It is detrimental to the baby to say things like, "Oh no – not another baby. We can't afford another child!" or "I hope it's a boy. I don't want another girl!" This is an open door for the "spirit of rejection" to enter the baby.

Heather: Baby in the Womb

One of our Walking in Wholeness Barbados team members attended an early childhood music program just prior to us meeting her in 2012. She got very excited about the course for pregnant women and believed the "baby in the womb" ministry was a call from the Lord. This was confirmed by two reliable sources. In December 2010, she began facilitating classes on Baby in the Womb at her local church and received further training in 2012 and 2013. At present, she is operating a community outreach centre for pregnant mothers and babies from three months to four years of age. We know that the baby's spirit in the womb hears what people say around a pregnant woman, and the spirit retains memories from the womb.

*The enemy is sneaky.
He will try to get to us in any way possible.
He wants to get back at God.*

- *Gender confusion*, whether from words spoken over us in the womb or the way we were raised as children, is another entry point for the spirit of rejection. If God created us female, He wanted us to be female. If God created us male, He wanted us to be male! Anything else is a learned behaviour. If we have questions about our sexuality, we should seek help and repent for rejecting the gender God created us to be. Scripture says God wove us together secretly inside our mothers' wombs.

For You did form my inward parts; You did knit me together in my mother's womb. I will confess and praise You for You are fearful and wonderful and for the awful wonder of my birth! Wonderful are Your works, and that my inner self knows right well. My frame was not hidden from You when I was being formed in secret [and] intricately and curiously wrought [as if embroidered with various colours] in the depths of the earth [a region of darkness and mystery].

♥ Psalm 139:13–15 AMP

- A *difficult birth* can be an open door for trauma and fear to come in. It can affect the newborn baby, and it is an open door for the spirit of fear to enter the baby. It also opens the way for a "spirit of death", a "spirit of destruction", or a "spirit of infirmity" because of all the activity in a delivery room.

- If we are left *alone in hospital* as a child while our parents go home, we may feel abandoned. This is an entry point for the "spirit of abandonment".

- As children, we could have associated *visits to the doctor* with getting a needle or the sound of the instruments in a dental facility, may have made us think of pain. Both can be entry points for the "spirit of fear."

- If we are *separated from our parents*, the enemy can enter and bring "spirits of abandonment, rejection, and/or fear". *Adoption* is an open door for "spirits of self-rejection, self-hatred, unloving, and self-pity". *Divorce* is an entry point for "spirits of rejection, abandonment, unloving/rejection, or insecurity". Often we blame ourselves, so "spirits of self-accusation and self-blame" can come in. Loss of a parent is very traumatic to the child! A "spirit of insecurity, abandonment, and/or anger" can enter through this open door.

These are just a few of life's experiences that could be open doors or entry points for spirits to come into our lives. These examples might show which spirits are affecting you. Ask the Holy Spirit to help you see the relevant things that have happened in your life.

Everything begins with a thought! Ask yourself,

 "Who told me that?"

If we agree with the thoughts that are coming from the enemy, we will open doors for the enemy to come into our lives. The goal is to establish the Kingdom of Heaven in our lives and not be bound to sin that will bring in all the accompanying curses. Galatians 5:1 tells us, "We have freedom now, because Christ made us free." So stand strong in that freedom. Don't go back into slavery again. Don't worry or fret. Love and walk in forgiveness. These are the keys to staying free. The enemy will try every way he can and use every trick he can to get to us, in order to get back at God!

I can do all things through Christ who strengthens me.
♥ Philippians 4:13 NKJV

General Confession Prayer

Heavenly Father, I bow in worship and praise before you. I believe you love me unconditionally, and nothing can separate me from your love, through Jesus Christ, our Lord and Saviour. You have qualified me through Jesus Christ to participate in your family and share Jesus's inheritance. You have seated me in Heaven with Jesus. In His name I share His authority.

Lord Jesus Christ, I believe that you are the Son of God, that you are the Messiah come in flesh to destroy the works of the devil. I believe you died on the cross for my sins and rose again from the dead.

Father, I now confess all of my sins and repent. I now ask you to forgive me and cleanse me in Jesus's blood. I believe that His blood cleanses me continually from all sin. Thank you for redeeming me, cleaning me, justifying me, and sanctifying me. In Jesus's name.

Warfare Prayer

I cover myself with the blood of the Lord Jesus Christ as my protection. I surrender myself completely and unreservedly in every area of my life to you. I take a stand against all the workings of Satan's kingdom that would hinder me in my prayer life. I address myself only to the true and living God and refuse any involvement of Satan's kingdom in my prayer. Satan's kingdom, I command you, in the name of our Lord Jesus Christ, to leave my presence with all your demons. I bring the blood of the Lord Jesus Christ between us. I resist all the endeavours of wicked spirits to rob me of the will of God. I choose to be transformed by the renewing of my mind. I pull down all the strongholds of Satan's kingdom.

Forgiveness Prayer

Lord, I have a confession to make: I have not always loved but have resented certain people and have unforgiveness in my heart, and I call upon you, Lord, to help me forgive them. It is my will and desire to forgive them from my heart. I don't know if I can, but I choose to, in Jesus's name. I ask you to help me forgive them and take all of the hurt and pain away. I do now forgive (name them, both living and dead) and ask you to forgive them also, Lord. I do now forgive and accept myself, in the name of Jesus Christ.

If you find yourself having a difficult time forgiving someone, please read the prayer below:

Unforgiveness Prayer

I find at this time I cannot forgive (name the person or persons) because it hurts too much. I know you want me to forgive them, Lord, and I ask you to help me to do so. Take the hurt and the unforgiving spirit away, and help me to forgive them truly. In Jesus's name I pray. Amen.

Forgiveness is not for the other person.
It is for you.
Walking in forgiveness will set you free!

Note: The scientific information in this chapter is based on the research of Dr Caroline Leaf.

Chapter Six

WHERE THERE IS
LOVE,THERE IS LIFE!

EVERYTHING IN LIFE HAS A purpose. Understanding the inherent God–given purpose for the male and female will enlighten our understanding of our spouses. It's important to understand why we get married and how God plays an important role in our marriages. When there is love in marriage, things go smoothly, and everything in life has purpose.

In Genesis 2, God declares it is not good for Adam (the first man) to live alone, so, in a special act of creation, He makes a woman, and Adam calls her his "wife". Eden is the scene of the first marriage, ordained by God Himself. "A man leaves his father and mother and is united to his wife, and they become one flesh" (Genesis 2:24).

God's Design for Marriage

God's design for marriage involves a man and a woman. God ordained that sex only take place between a married couple and that a family unit be formed when a man and woman come together in a sexual relationship and have children. God's design for marriage is that it is intended to last for a lifetime. Because the bond is "in the flesh", we are designed to be together forever. God designed marriage for life. When a man and a woman make a commitment to marry, they become one flesh. God's design for marriage is monogamy. Even though some people in Scripture did have multiple wives, it is clear from the account of the Creation that God's design for marriage was one man and one woman.

> But Jesus said to them, "Because of your hardness of heart your condition of insensibility to the call of God he wrote you this precept in your Law. But from the beginning of creation God made them male and female. For this reason a man shall leave [behind] his father and his mother and be joined to his wife and cleave closely to her permanently, and the two

shall become one flesh, so that they are no longer
two, but one flesh. What therefore God has united
(joined together), let not man separate or divide."
♥ Mark 10:5–9 AMP

Let's discuss marriage the way that God has designed it to be. Scripture says that marriage is sacred and binding. Is it possible for marriage to be like Heaven on Earth? *Yes!* Father God has a plan and has set up an order, which is a government in heaven, and on earth, and in marriage. Have you heard it said, "If Mama isn't happy, then nobody is happy."? Well, that's ungodly order. The husband sets the home in order, not the wife. Godly order happens when a man is under God, and his wife finds safety, peace, and happiness under the covering of the husband.

Agape love is so important.

The head of every man is Christ. As Christ came to show us the Father, so we, as men, are to download the Father's heart through Christ to our sisters in society. When we are born male, that comes with the territory. We don't have a choice! Also, the head of every woman is the man. The head of Christ is God. The spiritual head of the woman is man, submitted to Christ, who does the will of the Father. That provides true security for the woman. That is a man's calling, so he needs to accept it. That is who he is. Christ is the head of every man. The head of the woman is her husband, and the head of Christ is God.

The *husband* is the spiritual head of the woman – not the boyfriend or person she lives with! The husband must also be a born-again Christian to be the spiritual leader of the woman or wife. Let's have no misunderstanding about that.

But I want you to know that the head of every man is Christ, the head of woman is man, and the head of Christ is God.

♥ 1 Corinthians 11:3 NKJV

God's Formula for Marriage

God's formula for marriage is *1 + 1 = 1*. When a husband and wife begin to have one mind in line with the Word, God is able to make amazing things happen, because they are joined together in faith and unity. The Godhead has an order too. Jesus said He only did the things that He saw His Father do and only said the things He heard His Father say. God the Father directed Jesus, and Jesus was in agreement with His Father. This is the template from heaven for us to model in marriage. It's important to really communicate in a marriage! Sometimes we think it is more "spiritual" to be silent, but that's not true. God is very expressive and shows us in the Word that He has a lot to share! The Lord says in His Word that if we don't have love, we are empty (shallow). It is very important if we are born-again Christians that we marry other born-again Christians, because Scripture tells us not to be unequally yoked. This has nothing to do with the colour of our skin.

> *The husband should give to his wife her conjugal*
> *rights (goodwill, kindness, and what is due her as*
> *his wife), and likewise the wife to her husband. For*
> *the wife does not have [exclusive] authority and*
> *control over her own body, but the husband [has*
> *his rights]; likewise also the husband does not have*
> *[exclusive] authority and control over his body, but*
> *the wife [has her rights]. Do not refuse and deprive*
> *and defraud each other [of your due marital rights],*
> *except perhaps by mutual consent for a time, so that*
> *you may devote yourselves unhindered to prayer.*
> *But afterwards resume marital relations, lest Satan*
> *tempt you [to sin] through your lack of restraint of*
> *sexual desire.*
>
> ♥ 1 Corinthians 7:3–5 AMP

Men and woman are equal in God's eyes. Godly order provides a way for both genders to function the way He created them to function. Women need a safe place to learn to be vulnerable. Men need to learn to create a safe place by leading with strength and compassion in the home. It is a journey. When we, as men and women, express our weaknesses to Father God, we can learn and grow together. Marriage is honourable among all and the bed undefiled. God will judge fornication and adultery.

> *For [of course] every house is built and furnished*
> *by someone, but the Builder of all things and the*
> *Furnisher [of the entire equipment of all things]*

is God. And Moses certainly was faithful in the administration of all God's house [but it was only] as a ministering servant. [In his entire ministry he was but] a testimony to the things which were to be spoken [the revelations to be given afterward in Christ].

♥ Hebrews 3:4–5 AMP

What about Divorce?

The Pharisees were asking Jesus about divorce. Jesus said, "Moses wrote that command for you, because you refused to accept God's teaching, but when God made the world, He made people male and female." That is why a man will leave his father and mother and be joined to his wife, and the two people will become one. God has joined them together, so no one should separate them.

It has also been said, whoever divorces his wife must give her a certificate of divorce. But I tell you, whoever dismisses and repudiates and divorces his wife, except on the grounds of unfaithfulness (sexual immorality), causes her to commit adultery, and whoever marries a woman who has been divorced commits adultery.

♥ Matthew 5:31–32 AMP

Any man or woman who divorces his spouse must give a written notice of divorce. But if the divorce is for any other reason than sexual immorality, it will cause the other person (husband or wife) to be guilty of adultery. This is the only instance in the Bible that I see where someone can cause another person to sin. I believe, in this case, that the person who caused the person to commit adultery is responsible for that sin, so the curse will go on them. What the Lord is telling us is that we must work things out, because the Lord hates divorce.

Principles of Marriage

1. Because of sexual immorality, let each man have his own wife, and let each woman have her own husband.

2. Let the husband render to his wife the affection due her, and likewise also the wife to her husband.

3. The wife does not have authority over her own body, but the husband does. And likewise, the husband does not have authority over his own body, but the wife does.

4. Do not deprive one another except with consent for a time, that you may give yourselves to fasting and prayer; and come together again so that

Satan does not tempt you because of your lack of self-control.

Adultery starts in the heart.

Our marriage vows before God mean that neither the husband, nor the wife, nor anyone else can separate the two joined in holy matrimony (Mark 10:6-9). When God brings a man and woman together, and they choose to separate or divorce, they are in disobedience which is sin. The Lord said the only permission for divorce is when a person in a marriage commits adultery. When we have unconditional love in our lives and marriages, we will stay together and bond together. The Word of God is truth. Let's not allow Satan to come into our lives or our marriages. Marriage is too precious and important. When we obey God, we will walk in love in our marriages and in His blessings. "God does not lie."

For I am the Lord, I do not change; that is why you, O sons of Jacob, are not consumed.

♥ Malachi 3:6 AMP

What about Submission?

Submission is an important issue in marriage. "Wives, submit yourselves to your own husbands as you do to the Lord. For the husband is the head of the wife, as Christ is the head of the church, His body, of which He is the Saviour. Now as the church submits to Christ, so also wives should submit to their husbands in everything" (Ephesians 5:22–24). Submission is not a reflection of inferiority. Christ always submitted Himself to the will of His Father without giving up His worth (Luke 22:42; John 5:30).

A wife is to willingly submit to her husband in personal obedience to the Lord Jesus. She submits to her husband because she loves Jesus. The example of a wife's submission is that of the Church to Christ. There is nothing said of the wife's abilities, talents, or worth; the fact that she submits to her own husband does not imply that she is inferior or less worthy in any way.

Wives, likewise, be submissive to your own husbands, that even if some do not obey the word, they, without a word, may be won by the conduct of their wives, when they observe your chaste conduct accompanied by fear. Do not let your adornment be merely outward – arranging the hair, wearing gold, or putting on fine apparel – rather let it be the hidden person of the heart, with the incorruptible beauty of a gentle and quiet spirit, which is very precious in the sight of God. For in this manner, in former times, the holy women who trusted in God also adorned themselves, being submissive to their own husbands, as Sarah obeyed Abraham, calling him lord, whose daughters you are if you do good and are not afraid with any terror. Husbands, likewise, dwell with them with understanding, giving honour to the wife, as to the weaker vessel, and as being heirs together of the grace of life, that your prayers may not be hindered. Finally, all of you be of one mind, having compassion for one another; love as brothers, be tenderhearted, be courteous; not returning evil for evil or reviling for reviling, but on the contrary blessing, knowing that you were called to this, that you may inherit a blessing. For he who would love life and see good days, let him refrain his tongue from evil, and his lips from speaking deceit.

♥ 1 Peter 3:1–10 NKJV

Submission should be a natural response to loving relationship. When a husband loves his wife as Christ loves the Church (Ephesians 5:25–33), submission is a natural response from a wife to her husband. A wife should submit to her husband, not because women are inferior but because that is how God designed the marital relationship to function.

 Marriage is sacred and binding.

God says not to let the sun go down on our wrath. In other words, we should not go to bed with anger in our hearts toward our spouses. God tells us to settle any situations before we go to bed. This is very important. If we don't settle things, Satan has a chance to get a foothold in our lives (Ephesians 4:26-27). We should always walk in love and forgiveness.

God has given us the above principles for a healthy marriage, and going against His principles, is sin. We can come into agreement with the Lord by saying the following prayer and allow the love to flow into us and through our marriages. Let us forgive each other and forget the past, so we can enjoy marriages that are blessed by God.

Prayer

Heavenly Father, I repent and come to you admitting that I am a sinner. Right now, I choose to turn away from sin (name the sin that has come between you and your spouse), and I ask you to cleanse me of all unrighteousness. I believe that your Son, Jesus Christ, died on the cross to take away my sins. I also believe that He rose from the dead so that I might be forgiven of my sins and be made righteous through faith in Him. I call on the Name of Jesus Christ to be the Saviour and Lord of my life. Jesus, I choose to follow you and ask that you fill me with the power of the Holy Spirit. I declare that I am a child of God. I am free from sin and am full of the righteousness of God. I am saved in Jesus's name. Amen.

A happy marriage is the union
of two good forgivers.

Chapter Seven

WATCH YOUR WORDS!

WHY IS IT SO IMPORTANT to watch our words? Words are so potent that they can move us to tears, evoke joy in our hearts, or direct us to action. Our words have power – we need to use them wisely. Our words can mean life or death. They are blocks to build our lives and our future. What we speak will affect our future. We must learn to stop saying, "I wish" and start saying, "I will" – to stop speaking the problem and start speaking the end result, believing it has already happened. When we thank Jesus for healing us, and we believe it is already done, the healing will come. God will heal us; He wants to heal us, and He also wants to prevent us from being sick (3 John 2). God's will and our words work together. God always wants us to be healed.

> *A good man out of the good treasure of his heart brings forth good; and an evil man out of the evil treasure of his heart brings forth evil. For out of the abundance of the heart his mouth speaks.*
> ♥ Luke 6:45 NKJV

Healthy Words

Our own words can change our immune systems for better or worse (James 3:2–7). Our words are vital to our health and our well-being. When we speak God's Word in faith, we can build up our immune systems, eliminating sickness and disease - God's way. Our words can either be a blessing or a curse in our lives. It is very important to watch what we say, because we can speak our future.

Praying Words

God is loving and gracious. Our goal is to fulfil our calling as God's ambassadors in the world. As ambassadors, we cannot be effective without faith and without prayer. Praying is our way of communicating with our Heavenly Father, and His desire is to answer our prayers. Jesus used a practical approach in talking with His Father. When He prayed, He expected to be heard. He told us this in the following passage:

> *So they took away the stone. And Jesus lifted up His eyes and said, Father, I thank You that You have heard Me. Yes, I know You always hear and listen to Me, but I have said this on account of and for the benefit of the people standing around, so that they may believe that You did send Me [that You have made Me Your Messenger].*
>
> ♥ John 11:41–42 AMP

Jesus gave us an example for prayer. When Jesus spoke, He always used faith-filled words, so it is important to follow His example when we speak and when we pray. He said to one woman: "Your faith has made you whole." It's important that we pray every day. Sometimes special prayer is needed to focus on certain issues or events. God instituted prayer as a way of communicating with Him, and He answers prayer according to His perfect timing. That is why Jesus told His disciples that they should always pray and never give up (Luke 18:1). Jesus gave us the assurance that God is faithful in answering our prayers. Why is it important to talk about prayer here? We are talking about our words, and our words in prayer need to be faith-filled; we need to believe in the end result. It is important to pray Scripture as well, because Scripture contains faith-filled words. We shouldn't be asking God to do what Jesus has already done for us. We should command it to happen, believing that it will happen. When we pray, we speak into existence what Jesus has already done (e.g. healing and deliverance) and expect it to be done.

> *For this reason I am telling you, whatever you ask for in prayer, believe (trust and be confident) that it is granted to you, and you will [get it].*
>
> ♥ Mark 11:24 AMP

Faith-Filled Words

Our Creator's obligation and commitment to sustain His creation shows us that we need to transfer our priority from our basic human needs to the priority of cultivating and maintaining a healthy relationship with God, with people, and with His Kingdom. What does this have to do with Creation? Here is God's answer:

> *Therefore do not worry and be anxious, saying, What are we going to have to eat? or, What are we going to have to drink? or What are we going to have to wear? For the Gentiles (heathen) wish for and crave and diligently seek all these things, and your heavenly Father knows well that you need them all. But seek (aim at and strive after) first of all His kingdom and His righteousness (His way of doing and being right), and then all these things taken together will be given you besides.*
>
> ♥ Matthew 6:31–33 AMP

The word "pagans" here implies that religion should not be motivated by the basic drives of human needs for food, water, clothing, shelter, and the like. Here Jesus states that God's number-one priority for us is to seek the Kingdom of God. This is the most important statement made by the Lord, Jesus Christ.

God talked about the important things, which are love, the Kingdom, and finances. Failure to establish correct priority causes us to waste our two most important commodities – our time and our energy. Jesus established God's priority for all mankind with several powerful and straightforward statements in Matthew 6:25–27. He tells us to put God's Kingdom first and not to worry about the things we need to live – what we will eat, drink, or wear. Life is more important than food, and the body is more important than what we put on it. Jesus gives us an example of the birds. They don't plant, harvest, or save food in barns, but our heavenly Father feeds them. He tells us that we are worth much more than they are. We will not add any time to our lives by worrying about these things. These statements imply that our self-worth is more important than our basic needs, and we should never sacrifice it for the sake of those needs. Speaking faith-filled words also over our lives and bodies is of significant importance. God's Word is the medicine spoken of in Proverbs 4:22 – the medicine to all flesh. Our words can change our immune systems for better or worse. We must speak faith-filled words over our health, our finances, and our lives.

Understanding the principles, concepts, and characteristics of the Kingdom of God will help us to enjoy all the benefits here on earth. We must learn how to act and think according to Kingdom principles, by always speaking faith-filled words. The Kingdom of God is in us, and it has to come out of us through our lives here on earth. God's Kingdom is one of love, righteousness, peace, joy, patience, and kindness.

> *But seek first the kingdom of God and His righteousness, and all these things will be added to you.*
>
> ♥ Matthew 6:33 NKJV

One of the goals for the Ministry of Walking in Wholeness Barbados is to see the Kingdom in and through people's lives here on earth. The concept of "kingdom" was not invented by mankind but was the first form of government introduced by our Creator. This concept appears first in the book of Genesis, at the creation of man. Man's original assignment from God was a "Kingdom" assignment. God said, "Let them have dominion over the earth." God's plan for man was to extend His Kingdom (government) to the earth through the principle of colonization. Man's assignment was to establish the influence and culture of heaven on earth by representing the nature, values, and morality of God on the earth. In this way, God's heavenly rule would manifest itself on earth through His extended image in mankind. This was the first Kingdom. Yahweh, the King, extending His Heavenly Kingdom to earth through His offspring, man. This is the wonderful message of the Bible. It is not a religion but a royal family in a life-transforming relationship with the Godhead.

Blessed are those who hunger and thirst for righteousness, for they will be filled.

♥ Matthew 5:6 NKJV

God's solution gives us a positive outlook and excitement in an easy-to-understand manner. I believe that humanity is crying out in search of a better world. God's plan, since Creation, is to have a relationship with us. We can't find that solution in religion or politics. The Bible is the only source. Its answers provide value, equality, significance, and purpose for all of humanity. God said He would give us an abundant life. We all can have that life through obedience and the understanding of God's plan for us. If we apply these principles to our lives – put them into practice – there will be change and transformation. These principles have been set in place by God for us and have been in place for centuries, until we can understand them and apply them to our lives. Then we can walk in the light and put the darkness of the evil kingdom behind. Praise the Lord!

Transformation is serious business.
Most believers are living
in the bare margins of what
God actually desires to do for them.
♥ Lance Wallnau

Jesus always did what his Father told Him to do. He loved and trusted His Father for guidance and wisdom. We are to do as Jesus did. He gave us the authority by His Holy Spirit.

*With men this is impossible, but with God **all things are possible**.*
♥ Matthew 19:26 NKJV

*If you can believe, **all things are possible** to him who believes.*
♥ Mark 9:23 NKJV

For with God nothing will be impossible.
♥ Luke 1:37 NKJV

Jesus preached that man can be born again, characters can be changed, and we can become new people in Christ. Life on earth can be beautiful! Solutions can be found. There is a light behind every shadow. There is life after death. Heaven and hell are real places.

No evil will befall me, neither shall any plague come near my dwelling. For you have given your angels charge over me. They keep me in all my ways.

♥ Psalm 91:10,11 NKJV

In the way of righteousness is life, and in its pathway there is no death.

♥ Proverbs 12:28 NKJV

Sinful Words

Can our words be *sin*? The answer is yes. If we speak evil words, that is sin. Scripture says we can sin in thought, word, and deed. Let's look at *thoughts*. When we are thinking of something that belongs to the evil kingdom, those thoughts are sinful, and we need to repent. Replace those thoughts with the things of God, things that are pure.

Whatever is true, whatever is worthy of reverence and is honourable and seemly, whatever is just, whatever is pure, whatever is lovely and lovable, whatever is kind and winsome and gracious, if there is any virtue and excellence, if there is anything worthy of praise, think on and weigh and take account of these things [fix your minds on them].

♥ Philippians 4:8 AMP

The same goes for our *words*. When speaking sinful words, we'll find ourselves operating in the evil kingdom. Our thoughts can become words. It is the same if we are *doing* evil things; we are operating in the evil kingdom. Let's be very careful and discerning about the evil kingdom. If we always operate in God's Kingdom, our words will be life-changing.

> If the power of life and death
> is in the tongue,
> only speak that which
> impregnates possibilities.
>
> ♥ Lance Wallnau

Faith-filled words spoken in a tone of love are life-giving. The Bible says in Proverbs 4:22 that God's Word is medicine to all our flesh. God's Word is the most powerful medicine available in the world today. Always speak the end result. Speak what you hope and pray for, because these will be faith-filled words. If your back is sore, don't say, "My back is killing me" – it will! Replace those words with "Thank you, Jesus, for healing my back. Thank you that it is already done." This is so important! As another example, instead of saying, "I don't think I can do that," say, "I know that with the strength and wisdom you have given me, Heavenly Father, I can accomplish all that you have asked me to do." Speaking in this manner has the potential to change your life for the better!

*What releases the future
comes out of your mouth.*
♥ Lance Wallnau

Thoughts and Words

In our pathway of life, there is healing and health. We *can* eliminate toxic thoughts that are operating in us. The Bible says we can sin in thought (thinking), word (speaking), and deed (action). Sin leads to death. Choose life! God Himself tells us to choose life.

When a thought comes into our minds, we may not think much about it. It may seem harmless. We might think our actions are more important than our thoughts, but it is actually the thought that comes first, before the action. Every decision we make, every word we speak, every action we take, and every reaction we have comes first from a thought. There are healthy thoughts and toxic thoughts. If we focus on our thoughts, whether healthy or toxic, it will affect our bodies, our feelings, and our spirituality. We must be careful of the thoughts and keep our eyes upon Jesus. What kind of thoughts are filling our minds today? What is hidden in our subconscious mind, waiting to come out of hiding and influence the decisions we make? What thoughts are replaying over and over in our heads?

Remember to ask yourself,

 "Who told me that?"

Casting down arguments and every high thing that exalts itself against the knowledge of God, bringing every thought into captivity to the obedience of Christ, and being ready to punish all disobedience when your obedience is fulfilled.
♥ 2 Corinthians 10:5–6 NKJV

The secret to a sound mind is guarding what sound enters your mind.

We must get our thoughts in order and get into the right frame of mind. Our thought life is very important. The average person processes 30,000 thoughts per day, so it is very important to renew our minds daily. We cannot do a single thing without first having a thought.

Do not be conformed to this world (this age), [fashioned after and adapted to its external, superficial customs], but be transformed (changed) by the [entire] renewal of your mind [by its new ideals and its new attitude], so that you may prove [for yourselves] what is the good and acceptable and perfect will of God, even the thing which is good and acceptable and perfect [in His sight for you].
♥ Romans 12:2 AMP

We must renew our minds daily through Scripture. Our thoughts take up space in our brains. Did you know that God designed us to control our brains, not have our brains control us? We must be very mindful of our thoughts. We are all thinking beings. God made us to think. Every time we think, we change our brains, for better or worse. As we think, we influence our brains. Our brains change while we sleep. The non-conscious or subconscious mind keeps all the data we collect. The more we use our brains, the more intelligent we become. Thoughts can even change our body physically. We are not victims of biology. Our minds control our matter. Hopefully, this will help get our minds on the right path as we become more aware of our thoughts.

Have you ever gone to bed thinking about something and awakened still thinking about the same thing? Have you been thinking toxic thoughts that you can't seem to get rid of, and they are taking up space in your mind and changing your attitude? You can stop this toxic thinking by focussing on the truth of God and living the life that God intended you to have. This is why our Heavenly Father tells us in Philippians 4:8 what to meditate and think on. That's the umbrella that we are to operate under.

The thought life is a garden
– it produces whatever is planted.
♥ Lance Wallnau

There is an old saying, "Sticks and stones may break my bones, but words will never hurt me." That is wrong! Words can be very hurtful and damaging, especially when spoken over us as children. I have counselled many people who were suffering over something that was said over them as children. Through counselling, we help people to get free from damaging or dangerous words that have plagued them all their lives. Words can make us sick and cause us to be dysfunctional.

There are no bones in the tongue, but it is strong enough to break a heart.

Words can bind and control and have an effect on every area of our lives. That's the reason Jesus told us to do everything "in love". Speak to people in love; whether you are correcting them or edifying them, always use love-filled words. If you speak to them in love, they will receive it. We were created in God's image, and He spoke everything into existence, and Jesus always spoke in love. God (when speaking to Jesus) said, "Let us make man in our image", and He did.

> *God said, Let Us [Father, Son, and Holy Spirit] make mankind in Our image, after Our likeness, and let them have complete authority over the fish of the sea, the birds of the air, the [tame] beasts, and over all of the earth, and over everything that creeps upon the earth.*
> ♥ Genesis 1:26 AMP

When God saw everything He had made, He said it was "good". When He made us, He said we were "very good". Elohim (God) also made man in His own image (Genesis 1). That has to be good, because God only has one measure to go by – Himself – and God is good. Look at how He values mankind (Matthew 6:25–26 and Matthew 12:12). These Scriptures tell us how important human life is to our Heavenly Daddy. Jesus (the Word) spoke the world into existence, and because He is in us and we are in Him, our words have power. It is very important to speak words that lift each other up. Our words are life. The Lord says that life and death are in the power of the tongue. We bless the Lord and Father with our tongues, and we worship God with our tongues. We can also curse man with our tongues. Our words will affect our lives.

We can speak words concerning our health. We are thankful for doctors who diagnose the problem, prescribe medications, and do surgery, but they cannot *heal*. God is the only healer, and His Divine healing is spiritual. It is administered through the human spirit (1 Corinthians 2:9–12). We must speak God's Word over our individual circumstance or situation. Every time we speak our faith, it creates a stronger image inside us. We must speak the end result or speak the healing as if it were already done, because Jesus took the stripes for our healing, and it *is* already done. It is included in the atonement.

Jane: Healing Testimony

Just prior to coming to Barbados with this ministry, I tore the cartilage in my left knee. It was very painful. The doctor told me that the only option for that was surgery. We kept praying over it and calling it back into alignment, calling the cartilage healed and believing that God had already healed my knee. By the time we left for Barbados, the knee was no longer painful. (I also believe that this was an attack of the enemy, because he does not want this teaching in Barbados.) A few years later, when God called us to move to Barbados to follow His plan for the ministry, we had to go back to Canada to sell everything and get organized to move. When we went home, my right knee was swollen quite badly and very painful. We saw the doctor, and he recommended a cortisone shot. I thought about this, and being aware of the damaging side effects of the cortisone shot, I chose not to take the shot but to believe in God for my healing. I knew I had the power to speak healing over my own body. Every time I took a step and felt the pain, I thanked Jesus for healing my knee and believed that it was already done. I kept speaking these faith-filled words, and in a little while, I realized I wasn't saying the words anymore! Almost two years later, I am walking without pain in either knee. God is good – all the time. He is faithful to His word. I thank Him every day for healing my body. I also received a diagnosis from the optometrist a few years ago that, according to medical science, is incurable and will only get worse. Each year I go back for my eye exam, and he doesn't really know what to say, because the tests show no advancement and even some improvement. This never happens. The last time I went to see him, he did not even mention the disease. I know that God has healed my eyes, and I know that my God will continue to heal my body. The devil is a liar. He keeps trying to bring me down, but I am aware of his attempts, and my God is faithful. Jesus took a horrific beating for my healing. He did not receive that treatment in vain. The healing is already done – just believe it and call it into being. I believe!

Psalm 103:3 tells us that God heals *all* our diseases. Isaiah 53:5 says that by His stripes we *are* healed. And in 1 Peter 2:24 it says, "by whose stripes you *were* healed." It's already done – we can speak it over our bodies. We can do the same for finances. Stop saying things like "I can't afford", "I'm poor", or "I don't have any money". We can call in the funds with our words. Say things like, "My God supplies all my needs", or "the finances are coming" – and believe that it is so.

> *With it we bless the Lord and Father, and with it we curse men who were made in God's likeness! Out of the same mouth come forth blessing and cursing. These things, my brethren, ought not to be so.*
> ♥ James 3:9–10 AMP

125

We have control over our brains. Neuroscientists have discovered that our state of mind (what our brains do) influences our overall mental and physical health. How our brains change is governed by how we use our brains. Intense mental focus and meditating on Scripture grows our minds, as opposed to our brains aging as we grow older. What we think influences every aspect our lives and the way we feel physically.

Life and death are in the power of the tongue ...
♥ Proverbs 18:21 AMP

Be sure you taste your words before you spit them out!

Let's be careful to watch our words, because our words can be sin. We have to change the way we speak; we should speak in love for the glory of God. Words are life! We can speak life over ourselves and over others. When we do so, God gets the glory, and we will have a beautiful, abundant, and healthy life in Jesus Christ.

Words have power.
Words can light fires in the minds of men.
Words can wring tears from
the hardest hearts.
♥ Patrick Rothfuss

Chapter Eight

DIRECT CONNECTION

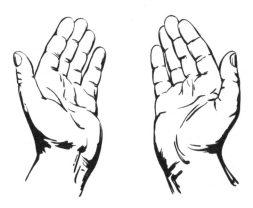

WE HAVE A DIRECT CONNECTION to Heaven that is free of charge, and there is never an interruption in the line. Our connection is prayer – that is how we communicate with our Heavenly Daddy. The most important thing born-again Christians can do is pray. We can plug into the power of prayer any time of the day or night. When we pray to God, we must believe that He will hear us and also believe that He will answer. Prayer changes things, starting with the person who prays. In order to receive from God, we must bring ourselves into position to receive. We come into position by believing – not doubting in our hearts or being double-minded or second-guessing ourselves (Matthew 14:28–32). The blessings that we will receive were already laid out for us when Jesus died on the cross on Calvary.

But let him ask in faith, with no doubting, for he who doubts is like a wave of the sea driven and tossed by the wind. For let not that man suppose that he will receive anything from the Lord; he is a double-minded man, unstable in all his ways.

♥ James 1:6–8 NKJV

We can hear from God by reading His Word and understanding it, by acting upon His Word and living it out, and by speaking His Word. We can hear from God through prayer, talking with our Heavenly Daddy and spending quiet time in our secret places, where we are alone with our Creator. God will also speak to us through visions and dreams.

Prayer is the very atmosphere of God's house.
As you engage in steadfast prayer,
you are building a habitation
for God's will to be done completely
in your life as a living temple of His Spirit.
♥ Lance Wallnau

Prayer is such a powerful force. Don't underestimate it. If we understood just how powerful prayer is, we would never feel hopeless. Prayer is a direct communication with our Heavenly Daddy. Nothing is too big or too small for God. He wants to hear all our requests. Sometimes we see or hear about things or people in the news media, and we become overwhelmed by their situation. We may feel we can't do anything, but we can pray. Even when I hear an ambulance or fire engine go by, I will say a prayer for the people in distress. We can pray short prayers all day long as we come across things, or circumstances, or people in our daily walks. We only need to say quick prayers. Let's learn to expand our circle of prayers beyond ourselves, our family, and friends and pray for other people: our pastors, political leaders, doctors, armed forces, etc.

Prayer is simply a two-way conversation between you and God.

♥ Billy Graham

God's Word and creative power is still just as it was in the beginning when God said, "Let there be light" and there was light. Spoken from our mouths and believing in our hearts becomes a spiritual force releasing His ability within us. God's love was there at the Creation. Genesis 1, verses 10, 12, 18, 21, and 25 tell us that God saw everything and it was "good". However, in verse 31, after He had made us in His image, God, in review, said it was "*very* good". You can see that God's love was there from the beginning. Genesis 2:7 tells us that our Creator breathed into Adam's nostrils the breath of life, and he became a living soul. God gave man his spirit (Ecclesiastes 12:7; Isaiah 42:5).

In Genesis 1:26–27, Elohim created man in His image. That has to be good, because only God is good. Let's look at the value of a human life.

Therefore I tell you, stop being perpetually uneasy (anxious and worried) about your life, what you shall eat or what you shall drink; or about your body, what you shall put on. Is not life greater [in quality] than food, and the body [far above and more excellent] than clothing? Look at the birds of the air; they neither sow nor reap nor gather into barns, and yet your heavenly Father keeps feeding them. Are you not worth much more than they?
♥ Matthew 6:25–26 AMP

Our heavenly Father is telling us something here – He loves us so much that He will take care of us, if we let Him. We are not to worry about anything, because worrying will not help. Worry can actually make us sick. God tells us to seek first of all His Kingdom and His righteousness, and all these things taken together will be given to us. We can bring all our concerns and requests to our Heavenly Father in prayer. God's timing is always perfect. If we think God is not answering our prayers, it is likely a sign that God is preparing something greater.

*Make an appointment with the Lord
and keep it.
A man is powerful on his knees.*

♥ Corrie ten Boom

Our Heavenly Father loves us so much that He gave His only begotten son to die for us on the cross, and He raised Him up on the third day to save us from our sins. Think about this. This is very exciting when you understand how much love is there – the sacrifice that was made! Think about it. Can you see what I mean? We are talking about human life and love.

How much better and of more value is a man than a sheep!

♥ Matthew 12:12 AMP

Sheep in those days were very valuable – that is why He uses the comparison. Jesus said, "So it is lawful and allowable to do good on the Sabbath", and He healed people on that day, because it was important. He loves us! The law stated that on the Sabbath they were not to work. That's how valuable we are to our Heavenly Father and our Lord and Saviour, Jesus Christ. *This is love!* He first loved us when we were still in sin. He has an unconditional, agape love for us. No matter what we do, His love for us will never change. He is the same yesterday, today, and forever. We can always talk to Him in prayer.

The words we speak will either put us over the top or hold us down in bondage. Many people have been held captive in their circumstances by their own words. The absence of God's Word in our lives will rob us of our faith in His ability. Mankind was created in God's image and in His likeness. When we speak His faith-filled words into our own situations, we will see our lives transformed, and God's creative power will flow from us. We can *have* what we *say*. Jesus told us in Mark 11:24 that whatever we ask for in prayer, and believe that it will be granted to us, we will have it. People tend to say what they have. When we delight ourselves also in the Lord, He will give us the desires and secret petitions of our hearts. We also have to put faith and effort to it, so it will work for us. Our Heavenly Father loves us, and He delights in us, and it is His pleasure to give us things.

Never underestimate the power of prayer. When you are praying according to God's will, your prayer is unstoppable. We know God's will by studying Scripture. Jesus made this promise:

> *If you abide in Me, and My words abide in you,*
> *you will ask what you desire, and it shall be done*
> *for you.*
>
> ♥ John 15:7 NKJV

Often we focus on the last part of that verse. God is not some sort of genie. The important part is "If you abide in Me, and My words abide in you". If we are walking in wholeness and fellowship with God and studying the Word of God, we will pray according to the will of God, and we will see our prayers answered.

> *Now this is the confidence that we have in Him, that if we ask anything according to His will, He hears us. And if we know that He hears us, whatever we ask, we know that we have the petitions that we have asked of Him.*
>
> ♥ 1 John 5:14–15 NKJV

Pray without ceasing, and don't give up or back down. That is why Jesus said the following:

> *Ask, and it will be given to you; seek, and you will find; knock, and it will be opened to you.*
>
> ♥ Matthew 7:7 NKJV

Take it to the Lord in prayer and wait to hear from Him!

Jesus' approach to prayer was also very practical. He didn't pray without expecting to be heard. At one point He said, "Father, I thank You that You have heard Me. Yes, I know You always hear and listen to Me, but I have said this on account of and for the benefit of the people standing around, so that they may believe that You did send Me and that You have made Me Your Messenger (John 11:41–42)." When Jesus raised Lazarus from the grave, He simply said, "Lazarus, come out (John 11:43)!"

Jesus told us that we can do the same things that He did – and even greater things. We must keep on speaking faith-filled words. Our words are building blocks on which we construct our lives and future. Our words set the cornerstones of our lives, and we live within the confines of the boundaries we create with our own words. Situations, circumstances, and conditions are subject to change, but with the support of our words, we can establish them in our lives forever.

The prayer offered to God in the morning during your quiet time is the key that unlocks the door of the day. Any athlete knows that it is the start that ensures a good finish.
♥ Adrian Rogers

Medical science confirms the Bible, and the Bible, both Old and New Testament, confirms medical science. Medical science tells us there are many incurable diseases, such as some forms of depression, cancer, diabetes, heart disease, and lung disease, to name a few. God's Word is supernatural, along with faith, when we speak it out of our mouths. God's Word is a creative power for healing even the incurable diseases! The world was formed by the Word of God. Confessing the Word of God will change our lives. We must allow God to change us from the inside out. This isn't something we need to fear but something we need to pursue.

Science is simply the discovery of what God has already done!

God declares that His Word will not return to Him void. We are to return His Word to Him by giving voice to it in prayer. For example, "I am free from unforgiveness and strife. I forgive others as Jesus Christ has forgiven me"; "For the love of God is in me, that agape love, and is shed abroad in my heart by the Holy Spirit (Matthew 6:12; Romans 5:5)."

We must put ourselves in a position to hear from God.

I assure you, most solemnly I tell you, if anyone steadfastly believes in Me, he will himself be able to do the things that I do; and he will do even greater things than these, because I go to the Father. And I will do [I Myself will grant] whatever you ask in My Name [as presenting all that I Am], so that the Father may be glorified and extolled in (through) the Son. [Yes] I will grant [I Myself will do for you] whatever you shall ask in My Name [as presenting all that I Am]. If you [really] love Me, you will keep (obey) My commands.

♥ John 14:12–15 AMP

At that time [when that day comes] you will know [for yourselves] that I am in My Father, and you [are] in Me, and I [am] in you. The person who has My commands and keeps them is the one who [really] loves Me; and whoever [really] loves Me will be loved by My Father, and I [too] will love him and will show (reveal, manifest) Myself to him. [I will let Myself be clearly seen by him and make Myself real to him.]

♥ John 14:20–21 AMP

Jesus answered, If a person [really] loves Me, he will keep My word [obey My teaching]; and My Father will love him, and We will come to him and make Our home (abode, special dwelling place) with him. Anyone who does not [really] love Me does not observe and obey My teaching. And the teaching which you hear and heed is not Mine, but [comes] from the Father Who sent Me.

♥ John 14:23–24 AMP

I love the Lord, because He has heard [and now hears] my voice and my supplications. Because He has inclined His ear to me, therefore will I call upon Him as long as I live.

♥ Psalm 116:1–2 AMP

O give thanks to the Lord, for He is good; for His mercy and loving–kindness endure forever! Let Israel now say that His mercy and loving–kindness endure forever.

♥ Psalm 118:1–2 AMP

Let those now who reverently and worshipfully fear the Lord say that His mercy and loving kindness endure forever. Out of my distress I called upon the Lord; the Lord answered me and set me free and in a large place. The Lord is on my side; I will not fear. What can man do to me? The Lord is on my side and takes my part, He is among those who help me; therefore shall I see my desire established upon those who hate me. It is better to trust and take refuge in the Lord than to put confidence in man. It is better to trust and take refuge in the Lord than to put confidence in princes.

♥ Psalm 118:4–9 AMP

The Lord is my Strength and Song; and He has become my Salvation. The voice of rejoicing and salvation is in the tents and private dwellings of the [uncompromisingly] righteous: the right hand of the Lord does valiantly and achieves strength! The right hand of the Lord is exalted; the right hand of the Lord does valiantly and achieves strength!

♥ Psalm 118:14–16 AMP

It only takes two to make a miracle
– God and you.

Chapter Nine

UNDER AUTHORITY

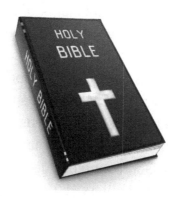

Why do people so consistently attack the biblical record and the plain truth about Jesus and His claims? In a word, it's all about *authority*. When the righteous are in authority – and the execution of the laws is in their hands for the protection of mankind and encouraging all that is good and discouraging everything that is bad – then the people rejoice because of the public good. People are happy under such an administration. Everyone feels and enjoys the advantages of it. When the wicked rule, people mourn and groan under oppression, and because of the sad state of things, the number of good men is lessened, and wicked men and wickedness are encouraged and promoted.

When the righteous are in authority, the people rejoice; but when a wicked man rules, the people groan.

♥ Proverbs 29:2 NKJV

Webster's Dictionary defines *authority* as "person(s) in command". There are principles of spiritual authority. Everything that God created must function under spiritual authority (Romans 13:1–5), and God is the source of all authority (Romans 13:1). Spiritual authority is given, never assumed. God says in His Word that spiritual authority to rule on the earth has been given to us through His chain of command. God's chain of command in 1 Corinthians 11:3 is as follows: God the Father, Jesus the Son, Church leaders, fathers and mothers (1 Timothy 2:12; Ephesians 5:22–23). We are either under authority or in rebellion. For example, Jesus said, "Not my will, but thine be done" (under authority), but Satan said, "I will ascend to the hill of God" (rebellion).

When you are arguing against Him
you are arguing against the very power
that makes you able to argue at all.
♥ C. S. Lewis

Many people today are suffering because of rebellion against their parents, and rebellion is sin. The Lord told us to honour our fathers and our mothers. Ephesians 6:1–3 is a Scripture that comes with the promise that if we honour our parents, all will be well, and we will live long on the earth. Our parents are the authority in the home and over our lives until we reach adulthood. We must respect our parents. This applies to anyone in authority, whether in the workplace, government, law enforcement, Church, etc.

You must know the difference between power and authority! There are two very important words in Romans 13:1–5. They are *subject* (stand under) and *resist* (stand against). Going against spiritual authority is rebellion (Romans 13:2). Do you know that sin is more easily forgiven than rebellion? If we reject God's authority, God will reject us (Luke 20:9–16; John 13:20). There are a lot of people doing their own thing these days. They do what they want even if it means rejecting God. These people are walking in sin, and they will be judged.

Three things must happen for spiritual authority to operate. It must come from God, be accepted by God, and be accepted by the people to whom Jesus was sent (Matthew 23:29; Matthew 10:40).

This is important!
When we reject God's authority,
we reject Jesus Christ!

We have two choices: either come under authority or rebel. If we continue to rebel, we will become blind and deaf to things of God. God's Kingdom does not accept rebels. People who rebel might say, "God said to do it" or "Jesus gave me an order". These rebellious people will always look to find something wrong with the authority that is in place rather than submit to it.

> *Let every soul be subject to the governing authorities.*
> *For there is no authority except from God, and the*
> *authorities that exist are appointed by God.*
> ♥ Romans 13:1 NKJV

Everyone must have a covering! Father God covers Jesus. Jesus covered Paul and is the covering for pastors. Husbands are covered by the Lord, wives are covered by their husbands, and children are covered by their father. People who are single (by death, divorce, or their own decision) are covered by the male leadership of the Church (or, for single women, their father, if he is still alive).

God is the source of all authority, and He does not give His promises to those who are in rebellion. Each one of us should look for someone to verbally submit to, so we can know the joy and blessings of spiritual authority. Submission is absolute, and obedience is relative. The only time we can go against authority is when it is unscriptural. We should not have a rebellious spirit; we should be obedient (unless it is not scriptural). The Word of God is the only authority that requires absolute obedience. When we live under this authority, life is more beautiful and appealing. We will be content with our lives, and everything will fall into place because of obedience and respect.

> His authority on earth allows us
> to dare to go to all the nations.
> His authority in heaven gives us
> our only hope of success.
> And His presence with us
> leaves us no other choice.
> ♥ John Stott

Obedient people who submit to authority are careful what they speak of, will never talk against the authority, and are always aware of rebellion around them. Does this mean that all people must think the same way? Absolutely not!

Scripture gives us examples showing how rebellion began, for example, Satan (Isaiah 14:12–14; Ezekiel 28:18–17) and Adam and Eve (Genesis 2:16–17). Rebellion is the spirit of Satan. Because of rebellion, woman were cursed (Genesis 3:16), and men was cursed (Genesis 3:19), and the ground was cursed (Genesis 3:17–18). The serpent was cursed and had to crawl on the ground on his belly all his life and eat dirt. That is what God told the serpent.

Satan will try to tell us that we can be equal to God, as he did while talking with Eve in the garden. If you try to be equal to God, it causes chaos. Do you know that rebellion actually begins with our thoughts (2 Corinthians 10:5)?

Ask yourself,

 "Who told me that?"

Recognize where the thoughts are coming from, take authority over them, and give them over to the obedience of Christ. What we don't control will control us! Our spoken words come from our thoughts. Rebellious thoughts will turn into rebellious words, but godly thoughts will produce faith-filled words (2 Peter 2:10–12; Jude 8–10; Ephesians 5:6; Matthew 12:34). We choose to put our thoughts into words, so we must be careful what we speak! The tongue is dangerous. It can direct the course of life, either the way of victory or the way of defeat.

And the tongue is a fire. [The tongue is a] world of wickedness set among our members, contaminating and depraving the whole body and setting on fire the wheel of birth (the cycle of man's nature), being itself ignited by hell (Gehenna). For every kind of beast and bird, of reptile and sea animal, can be tamed and has been tamed by human genius (nature). But the human tongue can be tamed by no man. It is a restless (undisciplined, irreconcilable) evil, full of deadly poison.

♥ James 3:6–8 AMP

As Christians, we can choose to live by reason or live by *revelation*. Jesus lived His whole life above reason! It is easier to live by revelation than it is to live by reason. Reasoning can become very complicated. If we argue with God, we have exalted ourselves to a position in which we think we can challenge God. The Kingdom of God is based on authority and obedience. Our King is Jesus Christ, and the Kingdom is government which has all power and authority.

And He went about all Galilee, teaching in their synagogues and preaching the good news (gospel) of the kingdom, and healing every disease and every weakness and infirmity among the people. So the report of Him spread throughout all Syria, and they brought Him all who were sick, those afflicted with various diseases and torments, those under the power of demons, and epileptics, and paralyzed people, and He healed them.

♥ Matthew 4:23 AMP

147

But seek (aim at and strive after) first of all His kingdom and His righteousness (His way of doing and being right), and then all these things taken together will be given you besides.

♥ Matthew 6:33 AMP

In God's Kingdom there is *absolute obedience*. Obedience is learned through suffering (Hebrews 5:8,9; Acts 5:32; Romans 20:16; 2 Thessalonians 1:8; 1 Peter 1:22). God will establish His Kingdom on earth with those people who operate in and under authority. The Church is God's authority here on earth and the foundation for the future Kingdom. "Thy Kingdom come, Thy will be done."

The Lord's Prayer

Pray, therefore, like this: Our Father Who is in heaven, hallowed (kept holy) be Your name. Your kingdom come, Your will be done on earth as it is in heaven. Give us this day our daily bread and forgive us our debts, as we also have forgiven (let go of the debts, and have given up resentment against) our debtors. And lead (bring) us not into temptation, but deliver us from the evil one. For Yours is the kingdom and the power and the glory forever. Amen. For if you forgive people their trespasses [their reckless and willful sins, leaving them, letting them go, and giving up resentment], your heavenly Father will also forgive you. But if you do not forgive others their trespasses [their reckless and willful sins,] leaving them, letting them go, and giving up

resentment], neither will your Father forgive you
your trespasses.

♥ Matthew 6:9–15 AMP

The Church must come under authority so it can exercise authority, such as the relationship between the body and the head. People cannot serve God without being under authority. They may survive by their cunning, but they will not truly prosper.

Rebellion begins in our hearts, but it is evident in our words and the way we speak (2 Peter 2:10–12; Ephesians 5:6; Jude 8–10; Matthew 12:24). Eve added to God's Word, and there is a penalty for adding to or taking away from God's Word.

I [personally solemnly] warn everyone who listens
to the statements of the prophecy [the predictions
and the consolations and admonitions pertaining
to them] in this book: If anyone shall add anything
to them, God will add and lay upon him the plagues
(the afflictions and the calamities) that are recorded
and described in this book. And if anyone cancels
or takes away from the statements of the book of
this prophecy [these predictions relating to Christ's
kingdom and its speedy triumph, together with
the consolations and admonitions or warnings
pertaining to them], God will cancel and take away
from him his share in the tree of life and in the city
of holiness (purity and hallowedness), which are
described and promised in this book.

♥ Revelation 22:18–19 AMP

Noah's son, Ham, rebelled by broadcasting his father's faults. Miriam and Aaron criticized and insulted Moses with their words, "Hath Jehovah indeed spoken only with Moses?" God places rebellious people in a class with animals!

But these [people]! Like unreasoning beasts, mere creatures of instinct, born [only] to be captured and destroyed, railing at things of which they are ignorant, they shall utterly perish in their [own] corruption [in their destroying they shall surely be destroyed].

♥ 2 Peter 2:12 AMP

We cannot live by reason. If God asks us to do something, and we don't understand why He is asking us to do it, we may disobey God if we try to reason it out in the natural. God's thoughts are high above our thoughts. God doesn't need to consult with us or get our approval (Romans 9:16–20). The Apostle Paul had a genius mentality. He had a huge capability for reasoning, and he lived in a dimension of reasoning in the natural – until he met Jesus on the road to Damascus. His first words were of obedience: "Lord, what wilt thou have me do?" (Acts 9:6).

Our words are spoken after we make a decision to express our thoughts. It doesn't make sense to say, "I spoke without thinking." It is impossible to speak without the decision process happening within the brain. One day we will have to give account for every word that is idle!

What about *delegated authority* – and what does that mean? Delegated authority is when someone in authority has chosen someone else to take that authority for a specific time or place. Jesus delegated authority to the disciples to combat disease, sickness, and evil spirits. They were successful because they were given the authority. They did not assume it. If we are born again in the spirit, Jesus has also given us the same authority. God has given authority to people by revelation. For example, Moses became the leader of Israel by revelation (Exodus 3:1–12), and Jesus became the leader by revelation: "This is My beloved Son … hear Him!"

> *"For I also am a man subject to authority, with soldiers subject to me. And I say to one, 'Go,' and he goes; and to another, 'Come,' and he comes; and to my slave, 'Do this,' and he does it." When Jesus heard him, He marvelled and said to those who followed Him [who adhered steadfastly to Him, conforming to His example in living and, if need be, in dying also], "I tell you truly, I have not found so much faith as this with anyone, even in Israel."*
> ♥ Matthew 8:9–10 AMP

If we are operating in submission to spiritual authority, we will have proof (fruit). The fruit is *life*! In Numbers 17, it is Aaron's rod; Moses invaded Egypt with a crooked stick and conquered Pharaoh. After God put ten plagues on Pharaoh and his people, Moses marched out with six million people. Now, that's fruit! Jesus took twelve men and invested within them the authority to establish the Kingdom of God. Those twelve men evangelized the known world and destroyed the devil's strongholds. That's fruit! If someone said to us, "God told me," and there was no fruit, we would know they lied! "By their fruits ye shall know them"!

> You can't be a city set on a hill
> and hidden at the same time.

If we are under spiritual authority, we will be humble and meek. We will love each other and make peace with everyone. We will not judge. We will be prayerful people, long-suffering and gentle.

> Humility isn't about avoiding
> the spotlight; it is about being
> personally unaffected by it.
> ♥ Lance Wallnau

Pride will keep us from operating under authority, so if there is pride in our lives and we want to be free, we can say the following prayer:

Prayer Confessing Pride

Father, I come to you in the Name of Jesus Christ. I know that pride is an abomination to you. You said in Proverbs 6:16 through 19 that there are seven things that are an abomination to you. You hate a proud look involving the spirit that makes one overestimate himself and underestimate others, a lying tongue, hands that shed innocent blood, a heart that manufactures wicked thoughts and plans, feet that are swift in running to evil, a false witness who breathes out lies (and sometimes under oath), and he that sows discord among his brethren. Father, I renounce these and turn away from them. I humble myself before you and come to you as a little child. I repent of all pride, religious spirits, haughtiness, ego, vanity, self-righteousness, arrogance, judging, criticism, and fault-finding. I ask you to forgive me of these sins and put them under the blood of Jesus. I repent of all judgements made in these areas and break all curses that result from these judgements and put them under the blood of Jesus Christ.

Come to Jesus Prayer

I come to you, Jesus, as my Deliverer. You know all of my problems (name them), all the things that bind, that torment, that defile, and harass me. I now loose myself from every dark spirit, from every evil influence, from every Satanic bondage, and every spirit in me that is not the spirit of God, and I command all such spirits to leave me now in the Name of Jesus Christ. I now confess that, through the blood of Jesus, I am redeemed out of the hand of the devil, and my body is a temple of the Holy Spirit, redeemed, cleansed, sanctified, by the blood of Jesus, and Satan has no place or power over me in the Name of Jesus Christ.

Authority exercised with humility and obedience accepted with delight are the very lines along which our spirits live.

♥ C. S. Lewis

Chapter Ten

LOVE THE SINNER?

HOW DO YOU THINK WE should feel about the person who is walking in sin? Should we love them or just disregard them? Jesus told us to love one another, but what about that alcoholic who is stumbling around, perhaps not well dressed, wearing shabby clothes, and perhaps smelling like rubbish? Is he a person, or is he just someone we toss out of our minds like a piece of garbage? Think about it!

Suppose a struggling alcoholic met you on the street and said, "Hi, my name is Fred, and I'm an alcoholic." What would come into your mind? First of all, let me say that this is just an illustration for the purpose of making a point, as most people would not do this, but bear with me here. What would you think?

Perhaps you would say, "Oh, he's an alcoholic; I don't want anything to do with him. What did he say his name was?" Or perhaps you would say, "It's nice to meet you, Fred. How can I help you? Is there anything I can do for you?"

Here's another illustration: What if Fred was sick with a disease such as cancer? If he introduced himself like this, "Hi, my name is Fred, and I have cancer", would Fred then be connecting himself with the disease or, as in the first example, with the addiction? Would he now be claiming the disease or addiction as something that belonged to him? "It's part of me." Would he be claiming it as his own?

We may have sin in our lives, or sin may be controlling our lives, but we *are not* the sin. The sin is a separate entity from us. When sin is removed from our lives, we are left behind alone – just persons, without sin and without disease! That's what Jesus did for us on the cross. Can we now distinguish between people and the sin that manifests through them?

Have you ever heard people say things like this: "I *have* cancer, and *my* cancer is in the bone", or "I *have* diabetes, and I have to watch my diet carefully", or "I *am* addicted to alcohol, and *my* struggle to get clean is really tough." I don't know whether you have ever been to a self-help group, but I'm sure you are aware of how they operate. In most cases, the program demands that they introduce themselves with their names and their problems or sicknesses, as in my example of Fred: "Hi, my name is Fred, and I'm an alcoholic." The purpose for this is to make people humble themselves and accept the fact that they are alcoholic or addicted – and it convicts them to *always* be addicted. According to Scripture, this is wrong! Jesus took the stripes for our healing. It is already done! The previous kind of approach offers no freedom and no hope for freedom.

You may have been diagnosed with a disease, but you *are not* the disease. Isn't that an awesome concept? When someone uses the words *mine* or *my* disease, or in the case of addiction, *I am,* they are actually claiming ownership of the disease or addiction. As Christians, we know that Jesus takes away our sins and heals us.

Beloved, I wish above all things that you prosper and be in health, even as your soul prospers.
♥ 3 John 1:2 NKJV

But He was wounded for our transgressions, He was bruised for our iniquities; The chastisement for our peace was upon Him, and by His stripes we are healed.

♥ Isaiah 53:5 NKJV

Who Himself bore our sins in His own body on the tree, that we, having died to sins, might live for righteousness – by whose stripes you were healed.

♥ 1 Peter 2:24 NKJV

What about Addiction?

Addiction is a sin, and most diseases are the result of sin. Someone may be living in sin, which could be an addiction (e.g. drugs, alcohol, gambling, work, pornography, etc.), or he or she could be living in the sin of anger, self-pity, bitterness, envy, jealousy, etc. or may have a disease that *developed* because of sin. *Is* the person the "sin" or "disease" resulting from sin – or are they a person who *has* a disease or is *affected* by addiction, or is *participating* in sinful actions? Another question: "If people are living in sin, *are* they the same as their sin?" If people speak to you in anger, are they the same as their anger, or did they *say* something that offended you? Are they the "action" (sin of anger), or is this a spirit of anger that is manifesting through them? When Fred said that he was an alcoholic, did that mean that he was *Fred* – or his *alcoholism*?

Love the Sinner, Hate the Sin

Separating the person from the sin is a major component in being able to defeat sin! When we can differentiate between the person (Fred) and the enemy (sin/addiction), we know what we have to fight. We can start to see what has joined us to the enemy, and we can separate ourselves or the other person from that sin! In order to overcome sin, separation is essential for the believer. Understanding this will set us free. Addiction is a spirit from the evil kingdom that is manifesting through the person. We should love the person and hate the sin. If a person is doing anything contrary to the Word of God, the Bible says, these actions come from the evil kingdom.

Wherever there is a human being, there is an opportunity for kindness.

We must learn to distinguish between the person and sin that is manifesting through him or her (or the disease and its consequences). Can we learn to separate the person from the sin? Can we love Fred and hate the alcoholism? Can we love the person and hate the sin? Whether it is an addiction, a sinful action, or a disease, the person is still the person, and the addiction, sin, or disease is a separate entity. We need to look at the person first and separate him from the sin, so we can learn to love the person and hate the sin. This is the only way we will be able to effectively help someone and minister to him.

We have to see the person for who he is as a person, not what he is doing, or how he is acting out, or what has happened to him due to disease or addiction. We have to separate the person from the sin; that way we can clear the pathway to deal with the issues and help him to walk in wholeness as God created him to be. Whether it be a friend who needs help, a member of your family or congregation, or Fred stumbling down the street, we need to separate the person from the sin; then we will be able to see the person who may be hidden behind the addiction or disease.

As He passed along, He noticed a man blind from his birth. His disciples asked Him, "Rabbi, who sinned, this man or his parents, that he should be born blind?" Jesus answered, "It was not that this man or his parents sinned, but he was born blind in order that the workings of God should be manifested (displayed and illustrated) in him. We must work the works of Him Who sent Me and be busy with His business while it is daylight; night is coming on, when no man can work. As long as I am in the world, I am the world's Light." When He had said this, He spat on the ground and made clay (mud) with His saliva, and He spread it [as ointment] on the man's eyes. And He said to him, "Go, wash in the Pool of Siloam" – which means Sent. So he went and washed, and came back seeing.

♥ John 9:1–7 AMP

From the cross, Jesus pleaded with the Father, asking Him to forgive his tormentors because they didn't know what they were doing (Luke 23:34). Jesus knew exactly who was behind his crucifixion. He knew it was Satan and the kingdom of darkness. Jesus then separated the thief beside him from his sin and forgave him, and the thief received salvation. Stephen, when being stoned to death, asked God to forgive his murderers (Acts 7: 60). Stephen knew it was the evil kingdom at work, manifesting through the people who were throwing the stones.

> *And falling on his knees, he cried out loudly, "Lord, fix not this sin upon them [lay it not to their charge]!" And when he had said this, he fell asleep [in death].*
> ♥ Acts 7:60 AMP

Where are we in our lives in terms of separating people from their sin? Can we love ourselves as God does and hate the sin? In cases where we've previously had trouble forgiving people, maybe because of their actions towards us, can we now choose to separate these persons from their sin, forgiving them and hating the sin? This does not condone what they are doing, but by separating them from the sin, we can see people for who they really are – and perhaps help them to get out of the sin they are walking in. Let's ask God to help us discern when it is the evil kingdom working in and manifesting through people. When we do that, we will know how to respond in love, to be able to pray positively over the situation or disease, to act with more wisdom, and to minister to people in a more effective way, in the power of God's love and the Holy Spirit.

Talk to those who are walking in sin
so you can to help them
to walk in wholeness –
God's way.

Chapter Eleven

THE GREEN-EYED MONSTER

Have you spent your life trying to meet the expectations of others? Perhaps from childhood someone has forced you to take on a personality, job, or lifestyle. Are you the person today that God planned you to be? Do you know who you are? Are you aware that jealousy, envy, and covetousness are "spirits"? These spirits are "green-eyed" monsters from the evil kingdom.

When we take our eyes off God and put them on a person, place, or thing, we have a "spirit of envy", a "spirit of jealousy", and/or a "spirit of covetousness". This is called idolatry, when we are worshiping a person, place, or thing instead of God the Father. God *will not* share us with any false gods or idols. Whatever we worship will become our god, and in His jealousy, God will release us to our own devices without any protection from Him. If an idol becomes our god, that god will have to take care of us. That's why it is so dangerous to take our eyes off Jesus and look to things of this world. It's not worth it!

Jealousy and Envy

Jealousy and envy are emotions we may all have felt at some time in our lives. If these emotions become dominant in our lives, they can put our perspective on life out of whack, keep us from realizing our personal potential and, in some cases, lead us into destructive behaviour. Without question, jealousy and envy will interfere with our spiritual growth. Another meaning for *jealous* is when God, the Father, is jealous for us, whom He has purchased by allowing His one-and-only Son to die on the cross for us. We have a covenant relationship with Jesus. When the apostle Paul was jealous for the churches, it reflected this same characteristic and relationship. God has every right to be jealous; He is meant to be the only God in the life of his very own creation (Exodus 20:5, Joel 2:18; Ezekiel 39:25).

For I am zealous for you with a godly eagerness and a divine jealousy, for I have betrothed you to one Husband, to present you as a chaste virgin to Christ.
♥ 2 Corinthians 11:2 AMP

There is a difference between jealousy and envy. Jealousy can be used in a good sense. Its root is the Greek word *zelos,* the same word from which we also get *zeal,* or *zealous.* When the Word refers to God, saying that He is a jealous God, it means that He demands that we worship and love Him exclusively. In a bad sense, jealousy is a fear of being displaced by a rival for affection or favour. *Jealous* means to be suspicious or vigilant. The main difference between envy and jealousy is that envy is an emotion related to coveting what someone else has, while jealousy is the emotion related to fear that something you have will be taken away by someone else.

Anger is cruel and fury overwhelming, but who can stand before jealousy?"
♥ Proverbs 27:4 AMP

Jealousy corrupts our motives, thoughts, and actions. The person who is the object of the jealousy may be unaware of it and unable to deal with it. While jealousy can be positive, as in the example of God being jealous, envy always has a bad meaning. The definition of envy is "a feeling of discontent and resentment aroused by another's desirable possessions or qualities, accompanied by a strong desire to have them for oneself." We may *envy* others for what God has blessed them with, whether it be riches or "stuff" that they have. As well, we may *covet,* which means a very strong desire or craving for what others have.

A sound heart is life to the body, but envy is rottenness to the bones.

♥ Proverbs 14:30 NKJV

There are two types of jealousy: a desire for what others have and a desire for what we do not have.

[And it is, indeed, a source of immense profit, for] godliness accompanied by contentment (that contentment which is a sense of inward sufficiency) is great and abundant gain.

♥ 1 Timothy 6:6 AMP

But if you show servile regard (prejudice, favouritism) for people, you commit sin and are rebuked and convicted by the Law as violators and offenders.

♥ James 2:9 AMP

When we *envy,* we may feel discontent or ill will for someone else's blessing or riches. We may even dislike the person for what they have. When we are *discontent,* we are not happy with what God has provided. We may follow the world and use credit cards or a line of credit to get what we want when it isn't within our budgets. *Comparison* is seeing other people's talents, or skills, or ability to do things that we struggle with – instead of understanding that we are *unique*. We all have different gifts. We need to be who we are, and be happy with who we are, as God designed us to be. We can always strive for improvement in all areas of our lives.

Julie: Spirits of Jealousy and Envy

Julie grew up in a very poor family and was ridiculed in school for the way she dressed. She was also of very small build and thin and was called "skinny" by her classmates. She always felt ashamed of her clothes and lived a life comparing herself to others; feelings of jealousy and envy filled her whole childhood and even her adult life. These feelings followed her into marriage and affected her relationship with people in the church and in the business world. It wasn't until she took the Walking in Wholeness course in Barbados that she realized that these feelings were actually spiritual. Through the course, she also came to realize who she was in Christ and how much her Heavenly Daddy loved her just the way she was. Through counselling and deliverance, Julie learned to be content with God's provision and the way He created her. She now walks proudly in wholeness, knowing that she is a unique creation in Christ. Her whole countenance has changed. She is glowing, and she looks beautiful. I would say that many people in this world probably envy her for her slim build. She walks with her head held high, proud of who she is in Christ; she has a beautiful smile and confidence in herself. She has come from a shy, quiet person to someone who now stands up in public and confidently speaks about Jesus. She goes on mission trips and works with young children.

Comparison is a work of Hell.
It leads to envy.
You are unique and are not
meant to be like someone else.
We need the gift and expression
that Heaven can give through you!
♥ Lance Wallnau

Not that we [have the audacity to] venture to class or [even to] compare ourselves with some who exalt and furnish testimonials for themselves! However, when they measure themselves with themselves and compare themselves with one another, they are without understanding and behave unwisely.
♥ 2 Corinthians 10:12 AMP

Traits of the Spirit of Jealousy and Envy

- *Covetousness*: not being satisfied with what God has provided and desiring other things

- *Pride:* source of envy. Comparing ourselves to others, always striving to do better, wanting to be martyrs or thinking we are better or higher than others

  Not given to wine, not combative but gentle and considerate, not quarrelsome but forbearing and peaceable, and not a lover of money [insatiable for wealth and ready to obtain it by questionable means].

  ♥ 1 Timothy 3:3 AMP

- *Self-Condemnation:* listening to thoughts coming from Satan that condemn us, instead of knowing that God created us and He said we were "very good"

- *Competitiveness:* always striving to do better than others instead of being content with who God made us to be

- *Treachery:* making plans to do harm to someone who trusts us

  Do not contrive or dig up or cultivate evil against your neighbour, who dwells trustingly and confidently beside you.

  ♥ Proverbs 3:29 AMP

- *Craving:* a strong desire for something (e.g. nicotine, alcohol, ice cream, pizza)

- *Curiosity:* trying to get more information than we need

- *Self-Pity:* feeling sorry for ourselves

Thank [God] in everything [no matter what the circumstances may be, be thankful and give thanks], for this is the will of God for you [who are] in Christ Jesus [the Revealer and Mediator of that will].
   ♥ 1 Thessalonians 5:18 AMP

- *Gossip:* putting others down to make ourselves feel better or building ourselves up in comparison to others. Talking about other people in order to experience life through the feelings or actions of others. Debasing the character of others is murder with the tongue. People who do this may also have poor self-esteem; they may compare themselves to others in an effort to be accepted.

You shall not go up and down as a dispenser of gossip and scandal among your people, nor shall you [secure yourself by false testimony or by silence and] endanger the life of your neighbour. I am the Lord.
   ♥ Leviticus 19:16 AMP

A perverse man sows strife, and a whisperer separates close friends.
   ♥ Proverbs 16:28 AMP

- *Discord:* disagreeing and being in conflict with others.

- *Not trusting in God:* borrowing money or using credit cards to purchase items that may not be necessities. This ties in with worshipping material things or people – for example, worshipping movie stars, which is *idolatry.*

We never have to compete for God's unconditional love in our uniqueness. God is no respecter of persons, according to Acts 10:34–35. When a spouse "cheats" on his or her marriage partner, the one being cheated on becomes jealous because of a promise the other made in the wedding vows. The covenant of marriage has been broken. "Fear of man" is when we think that others are better because of their position or title or even because of the material things they have, such as a house, car, or yacht. As well, we may have a twisted view of ourselves. God created each one of us different from the others. We are each *unique* creations. God made each of us individual and special in His eyes. When God completed His work (us), He said it was "very good", and if God says it is very good, it is very good. Be content with that.

And Peter opened his mouth and said: Most certainly and thoroughly I now perceive and understand that God shows no partiality and is no respecter of persons, but in every nation he who venerates and has a reverential fear for God, treating Him

with worshipful obedience and living uprightly, is
acceptable to Him and sure of being received and
welcomed [by Him].

♥ Acts 10:34–35 AMP

Often we lack boundaries; we spend more than we have because we are not content with what God has provided. We shop and spend compulsively, looking at things we don't need instead of keeping our eyes upon Jesus. Some people may steal other people's goods. "Kleptomania" is an abnormal, irresistible desire to steal items even if we don't need them. On the destructive side of this spirit, sabotage may come in; we may deliberately destroy, damage, or try to block something from happening. This comes out of retaliation and bitterness. We do things out of spite or wishing to hurt someone or make them suffer. People may talk about others in order to get one person going against the other. Satan's mission is to divide the body of Christ; destroy relationships with God, ourselves, and others; wreck marriages; break up families; and cause conflict between neighbours.

Scriptural Examples of Jealousy, Envy, and Covetousness

- Cain and Abel   ♥ Genesis 4:5
- Sarah and Hagar   ♥ Genesis 16:5
- Joseph's brothers   ♥ Genesis 37:4–11

- Saul to David   ♥ 1 Samuel 18:8–30
- brother of prodigal son ♥ Luke 15:25–32

Envy and jealousy can come into a person through sibling rivalry. As Christians, we must confront sibling rivalry. This can show up when there is a death in the family; for example, family members may fight and argue over who gets what. Long-term illness can bring envy and jealousy towards healthy people. If we are in a turbulent relationship, we could be envious of people who have a loving relationship. When someone gets a promotion, we may say, "Why not me? I can do a better job." When the spirits of jealousy and envy team up with the spirit of rejection, it can lead to addiction and sexual sins. Envy, jealousy, and covetousness all come from Satan and the kingdom of sin! To be envious, to covet, or to have jealousy is sin!

> *Now the doings (practices) of the flesh are clear (obvious): they are immorality, impurity, indecency, idolatry, sorcery, enmity, strife, jealousy, anger (ill temper), selfishness, divisions (dissensions), party spirit (factions, sects with peculiar opinions, heresies).*
> ♥ Galatians 5:19–20 AMP

> *And so, since they did not see fit to acknowledge God or approve of Him or consider Him worth the knowing, God gave them over to a base and condemned mind to do things not proper or decent but loathsome, until they were filled (permeated*

and saturated) with every kind of unrighteousness, iniquity, grasping and covetous greed, and malice. [They were] full of envy and jealousy, murder, strife, deceit and treachery, ill will, and cruel ways. [They were] secret backbiters and gossipers, slanderers, hateful to and hating God, full of insolence, arrogance, [and] boasting; inventors of new forms of evil, disobedient and undutiful to parents. [They were] without understanding, conscienceless and faithless, heartless and loveless, [and] merciless.

♥ Romans 1:28–31 AMP

For vexation and rage kill the foolish man; jealousy and indignation slay the simple.

♥ Job 5:2 AMP

Other Scriptures about jealousy and envy are Song of Solomon 8:6; 1Timothy 6:3–5; James 3:14–16; and Mark 15:10. When we are operating in the spirit of jealousy and envy, we can come down with sickness and disease, such as osteoporosis, colon cancer, and teeth problems (Wright, 270).

A calm and undisturbed mind and heart are the life and health of the body, but envy, jealousy, and wrath are like rottenness of the bones.

♥ Proverbs 14:30 AMP

A virtuous and worthy wife [earnest and strong in character] is a crowning joy to her husband, but she who makes him ashamed is as rottenness in his bones.

♥ Proverbs 12:4 AMP

When we are walking in wholeness, we will have the following:

- *a good relationship with God and He with us.* We will live our lives by showing the Father's love to everyone we meet. We believe His promises and have faith that He will provide everything we need. We accept who we are in the eyes of Jesus Christ and our Heavenly Daddy;

- *thankfulness* to be just who we are, accepting God's forgiveness and knowing that He made us all unique. We are all different from each other, and we accept how God designed us to be. We follow God's principles and are happy with what He has provided for us;

- *knowledge* that God is always with us. What more do we need? Let's choose to stay close to God, do His will, be filled with His Spirit, and overflow with the Living Word. Then He will give us the desires of our hearts;

Delight yourself in the Lord, and He will give you
the desires and petitions of your heart.

♥ Psalm 37:4 AMP

- *authentic love,* hating what is evil. We will only desire to do what is good and love each other in a way that makes us feel close to each other, like brothers and sisters, giving others more honour than we give ourselves and doing the best we can to live in peace with everyone (Romans 12:9–18);

- *eyes* that are focussed on God's Kingdom and have a desire to do only God's Will, knowing He will supply all of our needs (Matthew 6:33); and,

- knowledge that nothing is essential but God. We must never allow things to take God's place – not relationships, or financial goals, or specific material dreams about the future for which we have been suspending our happiness.

Let's look at our lives with the guidance of the Holy Spirit. We will confess, repent, and renounce any issue that is tied to envy, jealousy, and covetousness. We will submit and renew our minds.

And whatever you do [no matter what it is] in word
or deed, do everything in the name of the Lord Jesus
and in [dependence upon] His Person, giving praise
to God the Father through Him.

♥ Colossians 3:17 AMP

Do not let your hearts be troubled (distressed, agitated). You believe in and adhere to and trust in and rely on God; believe in and adhere to and trust in and rely also on Me.

♥ John 14:1 AMP

Love and righteousness are what Jesus Christ always taught in His ministry when He was here on earth and is still teaching us through the Holy Bible. Jesus said, "I leave my peace with you." He gives us joy, that joy that only comes from the Lord. This is the Kingdom of God. We should be living the Kingdom of God here on earth. When we have jealousy and envy in our hearts, we are not living in love. We are living in the flesh (evil kingdom).

Remember that God provides perfectly for us and that we are unique and valuable to Him. When we know this in our spirits, we will be better equipped to come against the spirits of envy and jealousy that try to make us compare ourselves, our possessions, or blessings to others. Only then can we be truly content with the things we have and be at peace, because we will know that He never leaves us nor forsakes us. That is how we overcome envy and jealousy in our lives.

Salvation Prayer

Heavenly Father, I come to you admitting that I am a sinner. Right now, I choose to turn away from sin, and I ask you to cleanse me of all unrighteousness. I believe that your Son, Jesus Christ, died on the cross to take away my sins. I also believe that He rose from the dead so that I might be forgiven of my sins and be made righteous through Him. I call on the Name of Jesus Christ to be the Saviour and Lord of my life. Jesus, I choose to follow you and ask that you fill me with the power of the Holy Spirit. I declare that I am a child of God. I am free from sin and am full of the righteousness of God. I am saved in Jesus's name. Amen.

Let's break the chain of jealousy and envy and get free, walking in wholeness – spirit, soul, and body!

Chapter Twelve

NEW WAY OF WALKIN'

(Walking Out What I Have Learned)

Aᴄᴛɪᴠᴀᴛᴇ ᴛʜᴇ ɢʀᴇᴀᴛᴇsᴛ ɢɪꜰᴛ ᴏꜰ *love.* We learn in 1 Corinthians 13 that if we speak in the tongues of men and even of angels but don't have love, we are shallow, like noisy gongs or clanging cymbals. And even if we understand all the secret truths and mysteries of the world but don't have love, we are nothing. Even if we possess all the knowledge and have enough faith to move mountains, if we don't have love, we are nothing. Without love we are just useless nobodies. That's how important love is! Even if we give everything to the poor and make all kinds of sacrifices, if we don't have love, we gain nothing. Love is patient and kind; love is never envious nor boils over with jealousy. Love is not boastful and does not display itself haughtily; it is not arrogant and inflated with pride. Love is not rude and does not act with disrespect. Love does not demand its own rights or its own way. Love rejoices when righteousness and truth reign. Love never fails and never fades out. We all need to have faith, hope, and love in this life, but the greatest of these is love. We know we have love when we can give it away, with energy, like Jesus Christ.

The following steps will help you to "walk out" what you have learned:

1. When you start something, finish it.

2. Walk in complete wholeness in a relationship with our heavenly Father and our Lord Jesus.

3. Keep working on what you have learned, and put it into practice.

4. Run the race that is before you, and never quit. Press towards the mark (Philippians 3:14).

5. Remove anything from your lives that is not of God.

6. Remember that when God forgives you, He chooses to forget.

7. You can't change the past, so leave it there, in the past.

8. Remember to forgive yourself and others, as God has forgiven you.

9. Always keep your eyes upon Jesus. He suffered death and shame on the cross just for you and the rest of mankind! Honour Him and always be thankful.

10. Persevere – it is the key to walking in complete wholeness.

Therefore then, since we are surrounded by so great a cloud of witnesses [who have borne testimony to the Truth], let us strip off and throw aside every encumbrance (unnecessary weight) and that sin which so readily (deftly and cleverly) clings to and entangles us, and let us run with patient endurance and steady and active persistence the appointed course of the race that is set before us.
♥ Hebrews 12:1 NKJV

Just think of Him Who endured from sinners such grievous opposition and bitter hostility against Himself [reckon up and consider it all in comparison with your trials], so that you may not grow weary or exhausted, losing heart and relaxing and fainting in your minds.

♥ Hebrews 12:3 NKJV

Spirit of Fear

Let's look at the difference between walking in *love* and walking in *fear.* When we are living in the *love* of Christ, we have the gifts of joy, peace, goodness, patience, kindness, faithfulness, godliness, self-control, etc. And the roots that establish a life of love and health include healthy thoughts, emotions, words, choices, dreams, faith, love, touch, and schedules. But when we are walking in *fear,* the opposite happens. We may have health issues, such as degenerative disorders, dementia, circulatory problems, migraines, etc.

Fear can affect the systems in our bodies, such as the immune system, central nervous system, cardiovascular system, digestive system, and also the mind, which may cause depression and/or bipolar disorders. Fear is often the root issue behind addictions such as drugs, alcohol, pornography, gambling, overeating, etc. Fear can cause stress, which may produce learning problems, such as difficulty in paying attention. We may become hyperactive and suffer from anxiety disorders, such as obsessive/

compulsive disorders, post-traumatic stress, panic, phobias, etc. And when we are living in fear, the spiritual roots which are creating havoc in our bodies include toxic thoughts, emotions, words, choices, dreams, faith, love, touch, and schedules – which may lead to toxic, unhealthy bodies.

Maintaining Freedom

- Start with the way we think, always keeping God's perspective in mind.
- Develop new and good Godly habits.
- Realise that every choice we make begins with a thought.
- Walk in the Holy Spirit, abounding in the Word, so we do not fulfil the lusts of the flesh.
- Have discernment of the tricks of the devil, the oppressor.
- Never voluntarily release the oppressed.
- Operate in the physical realm as well as the spiritual realm.
- Maintain the freedom that Jesus Christ brings.

It takes effort to walk in freedom, but God teaches us daily as we walk in His truth and read His Word. He will finish His work in us. That's hope!

*I [the Lord] will instruct you and teach you in the
way you should go; I will counsel you with My eye
upon you.*

♥ Psalm 32:8 AMP

*And I am convinced and sure of this very thing, that
He Who began a good work in you will continue
until the day of Jesus Christ [right up to the time
of His return], developing [that good work] and
perfecting and bringing it to full completion in you.*

♥ Philippians 1:6 AMP

His spirit is within you, so do not fear the battle. Just apply the victory of Jesus. God is mindful of each of us whom He has betrothed to His Son as a helpmate. When our spirit is healed, as we renew our minds, our bodies will follow and come into alignment with God's design. We are works in progress. We need to renew our minds daily. The Father has converted us from the authority of the dominion of darkness to that of the Kingdom of His Son. The goal is for us to become one with God in spirit, soul, and body. Our minds are to be renewed to think as Jesus thinks. We are temples of the Holy Spirit. Our souls are reflected in our spirits when we are joined to the Lord. We are spirit (Ephesians 4:23). Let us take every thought and imagination captive. Remember that temptation is just Satan's kingdom checking us out. The following Scripture is very important:

*Therefore, since these [great] promises are ours,
beloved, let us cleanse ourselves from everything*

that contaminates and defiles body and spirit, and bring [our] consecration to completeness in the [reverential] fear of God.

♥ 2 Corinthians 7:1 AMP

When a thought comes into your mind, Ask yourself,

 "Who told me that?"

If it is not a good thought, it is not from God.

And He said, "Who told you that you were naked? Have you eaten of the tree of which I commanded you that you should not eat?"

♥ Genesis 3:11 AMP

When we use these principles, we will keep our freedom in Christ.

Practise the following *R's* on a daily basis:

- *recognize* anything not from God;
- take *responsibility* for it;
- *repent;*

- *renounce* the sin and exercise your authority in Christ. Command evil spirits to leave, and send them into the abyss;
- *remove* the sin from your life;
- *replace* the sin with holiness;
- *resist*, and draw nigh to God;
- *rejoice* with thanksgiving in your freedom; and,
- *restore* others to God through Jesus Christ.

We receive deliverance from past hurts, wounds, and bondages, and we press on toward the mark. Understand that no matter what our nationality, or where we were born, we have a new citizenship in the Kingdom of God. We are no longer of this world. Our citizenship is in heaven, and we are just pilgrims passing through this world. Knowing this will help us to keep our focus on the goal. We should also note that the enemy is *not* going to give up. There will still be temptations, trials, tests, and attacks. When we are under an attack, we need to realize that "This too will pass". Everything in life is temporal.

Walk It Out

In discussing walking out deliverance, a couple of Scriptures relate. The first is in Matthew 12, verses 43–45, which concerns the dangers of emptiness. It tells us that when an evil spirit comes out of a person, it travels through dry places, looking for a place to rest. When it finds none, it says, "I will go back to the home I left." When it comes back, it finds that home empty, neat, and clean. The evil spirit goes out and gathers seven other spirits more evil than itself. They all go and live in the person, which causes that person even more trouble than before. It is the same way with the evil people who live today. We want to make sure that if and when that spirit returns, he will find the house full of the Holy Spirit and the power of God. To do this, we must be baptized in the Holy Spirit, and we must be full of the Word of God.

The second Scripture is the story of the man at the pool of Bethesda in John 5:1–15. In verse 8, Jesus said to the man, "Get up! Pick up your bed and walk!" The man was instantly healed. Following, in verse 14, Jesus found the man at the temple and said to him, "See, you are well! Stop sinning, or something worse may happen to you." Most bondages come in through sin; and most spirits and strongholds are fed by sin. So, to walk out our deliverance and to stay free, we, too, should go and sin no more!

Deliverance is a beginning – not an end!

We always need to walk in forgiveness. We must not let any root of bitterness spring up in us. Scripture tells us to pursue peace with all people (Hebrews 12:14). We also need to change old habits. I believe sin, as well as bad habits, opens the door for the devil to hook us into sin. So we need to ask God to show us any and all bad habits, so we can break them. To walk in freedom, we have to choose to walk in the truth of the Word of God and not by feelings. Feelings are up and down, and if we walk by our feelings, we too will be up and down. *Freedom is always walking by faith and in the Spirit.* Our testimony reminds us of where we came from and what God has delivered us from.

And they overcame him by the blood of the Lamb and by the word of their testimony, and they did not love their lives to the death.

♥ Revelation 12:11 NKJV

After Deliverance

After receiving deliverance, we should walk through our homes and clean out all the junk from the past. This means getting rid of all ungodly tapes, CDs or videos, books, pictures, magazines, letters, photos, knick-knacks, idols, witchcraft items, items relating to the Masonic Lodge (including jewellery) and, of course, any articles relating back to an affair or any ungodly relationship. Ask the Holy Spirit to indicate what may be in your home that needs to be removed. If you're not sure, get rid of it anyway.

For those who have not been baptized in water (immersion), this is something that must be seriously considered. Statics show that most Christians who backslide were never baptized. Baptism is commanded; it is not an option. Associate yourself with a good, Bible-teaching church and become accountable to someone like a group leader, pastor, or a mature brother or sister in the Lord. Start serving in the church.

On a daily basis, we should read the Word of God, pray, put on the full armour of God (Ephesians 6), and advance the Kingdom of God. We have to guard our thoughts and our hearts and ask ourselves,

 "Who told me that?"

We *are* what we *think*. We know that the battlefield is our minds so we must take authority over our thoughts, walk in freedom, and stay free! We should witness, testify, walk, and talk Jesus. We must refuse the thoughts that demons bring in and replace them with spiritual thoughts (Philippians 4:18). Bind the thoughts or attacks, and command them to leave in the name of Jesus.

Develop a life of continuous praise and prayer, which silences the enemy. Commit yourself totally to Christ. Determine that every thought, word, and action will reflect the very nature of Christ. Faith and trust in God is the greatest weapon against the demon lies. Maintain a loving spirit. Refuse to be hateful and mean, and confess love (Matthew 5:44). Maintain a forgiving spirit, because an unforgiving spirit is an open door that gives the enemy permission to come in and harass you.

And whenever you stand praying, if you have anything against anyone, forgive him and let it drop

(leave it, let it go), in order that your Father Who is
in heaven may also forgive you your [own] failings
and shortcomings and let them drop.
♥ Mark 11:25 AMP

Maintain a tender spirit. Stop being critical. Recognize when you mess up, and repent. Forgive if necessary, and command the spirits to leave in the name of Jesus. Learn to be a peacemaker, and exercise mercy and gentleness. You may have a lifetime of fleshly habits to be broken, but once the demon influence is gone, you will have the ability to attain victory. Yield to the love of Christ.

We must forsake sin, or a worse thing can come against us (John 5:14). If we slip up and fall, we must repent quickly, renounce the sin, and command any demon that is attacking to leave. Satan is the father of lies. Even though they are outside of us, unclean spirits can still talk to us (John 8:36). Satan is also called the "accuser". We may find ourselves feeling guilty for having had unclean spirits or for our past sins, and the enemy may try to intimidate us with demonstrations of his power. We may find ourselves tempted with old habits or behaviour that doesn't fit in with the Christian life. We need to recognize the enemy's strategy. Our enemy is not people we can see. We are wrestling against Satan and his forces of evil in the spirit realm. The enemy does not leave peacefully but must be driven out using the name of Jesus, who defeated Satan and all his demons at the cross.

Can a Christian Be Possessed by Demons?

I don't believe this to be possible. As Christians, we are filled with the Holy Spirit so no demon can possess us; however, we can be harassed by the demonic realm. That's why the Bible tells us to put on the full armour of God daily and to have discernment of the evil that surrounds us. When we agree with any evil force or any negative talk that has been spoken to us or over us, we open the door to be harassed by the demonic spirits.

We Are a Chosen Generation

We are overcomers. We know who God says we are. Our bodies are temples of the Holy Spirit – redeemed, cleansed, and sanctified by the Blood of Jesus. Our members (the parts of our bodies) are instruments of righteousness, yielded to God for His service and for His glory. The devil has no place in us, no power over us, no unsettled claims against us. All has been settled by the Blood of Jesus. We overcome Satan by the Blood of the Lamb and by the word of our testimony. We love not our life unto death. Our bodies are for the Lord, and the Lord is for our bodies. We're walking in miracles and we're walking in power. We live a life of favour. We know who we are in Christ.

Apply the following principles to your life:

- ✓ We are not just ordinary men and women. We are sons and daughters of the living God. We are joint heirs with Jesus Christ. We are part of a chosen generation, a royal priesthood, a holy nation. We are God's people.

- ✓ There is no condemnation for those in Christ Jesus. Thus we are not under guilt or condemnation.

- ✓ Satan is a liar. We will no longer listen to his accusations. No weapon formed against us can prosper.

- ✓ Our minds are being renewed by the Word of God daily as we read the Word. We pull down strongholds, tear down every proud idea that raises itself against what God says about us, and bring every thought captive to the obedience of Christ.

- ✓ We are accepted by God, and if God is for us, who can be against us? Nothing can separate us from the love of Christ.

- ✓ Satan is defeated; Jesus came into the world to destroy the works of the devil. He can no longer oppress us. Satan and all his demons are defeated by the Blood of the Lamb. As we submit to God and resist the devil, he has to flee from us.

✓ No temptation will overtake us. God is faithful. He will not let us be tempted beyond our strength, but with the temptation, He will also provide a way of escape, so that we will be able to endure it.

✓ We will not give any place to fear in our lives. What we fear will come upon us. Where God's love is, there is no fear, because God's perfect love takes away all fear. The Lord is our light and our salvation, so why should we fear? The Lord is our strength, so why should we be afraid? God is our refuge and our strength. He is there to help us when we are in trouble; therefore, we will not fear.

✓ We are proud of the Good News, because it is the power God uses to save everyone who believes.

✓ We are believers, not doubters. Our faith is not in ourselves or in our feelings but in a living God who will never leave us nor forsake us. We walk by faith and not by sight.

✓ We will be anxious for nothing, because God will keep us in perfect peace as we keep our eyes focussed on Jesus.

✓ We choose to live by faith, to walk by faith, and to see with the eyes of faith. We will go from faith to faith, from strength to strength, and from glory to glory.

✓ We look not to the healing but to the healer, Jesus Christ. Our bodies are to be used in service for the Lord, and the Lord will protect our bodies. Jesus already took away our sickness and carried *all* our diseases. By His stripes we are healed. The same spirit that raised Christ from the dead is at work in us, giving life.

✓ Christ carried our sins in his body on the cross. He did this so that we would stop living in sin and live for what is right. Jesus took a horrible beating so that we would be healed by his wounds (1 Peter 2:24).

✓ Jesus saw many people who had demons inside them. He spoke to cast the demons out, and they left the people. He healed *all* those who were sick. So Jesus made clear the full meaning of what Isaiah the prophet said: "He took away our diseases and carried away our sicknesses." Let's not lose the courage we had in the past. Our courage will be rewarded richly. We must be patient. After we have done what God wants, we will get what He promised us.

✓ Our love must be real. We hate what is evil and do only what is good. We love each other in a way that makes us all feel close, like brothers and sisters. We must give others more honour than we give ourselves.

✓ We work hard, are not lazy, and get excited about serving the Lord!

✓ We are patient when troubles come and pray all the time, in all circumstances.

✓ We share with God's people in need and look for people who need help. We welcome them into our homes and into God's family.

✓ We always speak good to those who treat us badly. We ask God to bless them, not curse them.

✓ When others are happy, we are happy with them. And when others are sad or hurting, we have understanding for what they are going through, and if possible, we help them.

✓ We are at peace with one another.

You're not the same person you were before.
Learn to be your own best friend.
Remember that God loves you!

Resources and Information
(used with permission)

Holy Bible, *New King James* and *Amplified Classic Edition* versions

Leaf, Caroline, (2009), *The Gift in You* (Southlake, Tx).

Leaf, Caroline, (2009), *Who Switched Off My Brain?* *(Southlake, Tx)*

Roberts, Rev Tim (2012), *"Walking in Wholeness" Basic Course Notes*, Health To You Ministry (Unpublished)

Sudduth, Dr Bill, (2010), *Deliverance Training Manual*, Righteous Acts Ministries (Colorado Springs, CO)

Wright, Henry W, (2009), *A More Excellent Way* (New Kensington, PA)

This book is based on studies and information from the above resources, along with my own Holy Spirit-inspired thoughts and information.

I asked, "Who is God?"
God said, "I am the great 'I am'.
I am peace. I am grace. I am joy.
I am strength. I am safety. I am shelter.
I am power. I am creator. I am comforter.
I am the beginning and the end.
I am the truth and the light."

Then I asked, "Who are we?"
God said, "You are mine".

Love and Forgiveness Is the Way

Preparing for an experience of love and forgiveness
and expanding the knowledge of God

*That you may have a walk worthy of the Lord, fully
pleasing Him, being fruitful in every good work and
increasing in the knowledge of God. Strengthened
with all might, according to His glorious power, for
all patience and long suffering with joy.*

♥ (Colossians 1:10-11)

About the Author

Pastor Errington Cumberbatch and Jane Cumberbatch are on the Board of Directors of Walking in Wholeness Barbados Inc., which is a Division of Health To You Ministry in Hamilton, Ontario, Canada. Errington is a Certified Pastoral Counsellor and member of the Canadian College of Christian Counsellors and the Evangelical Association for Education and Evangelism. They were married in Barbados, November 12, 2009 – a second marriage for both of them. They now live in Barbados and have dual citizenship in Canada and Barbados. God called them to bring the Walking in Wholeness teaching to Barbados in 2011 and, in obedience, they came there for the winter of 2011 to see if this was the Will of God. God immediately started opening doors and showed them very quickly that this was His Will for the Ministry. After three winters, God called them to move to Barbados and live for the next three to five years as missionaries. Their goal is teach this course in Barbados, to train and raise up a Barbadian team. This team will take it to the rest of the Caribbean, as prophesied many times by different people who did not know them. God has also laid it on their hearts to reach the youth who seem to be more influenced by the world and are turning their backs on the Creator. They have found favour with the Government of Barbados and have presented a pilot project to them to teach the Walking in Wholeness course in the schools. They are trusting God and are thankful for His faithfulness to provide.

For more information about the Ministry of
Walking in Wholeness Barbados Inc.
and
Health to You Ministry, Canada,
please visit
www.healthtoyouministry.ca.

If the Lord leads you to donate to help further the
Ministry in the Caribbean, you can find donation
information at www.healthtoyouministry.ca.

Please indicate that it is designated to the
Barbados Ministry,
or you can mail a cheque to
PO Box 3044
Holetown, St James, Barbados, West Indies.

Your support is very much appreciated.

Contact us at
246–424–6548 or 246–844–2443 or
email pastor@walkinginwholeness.today

Change your life with the power of love.
Love is everything.
It is life, and it is health.
We all have the "spirit of love"
which has been given to us by Almighty God,
our Creator and Heavenly Father,
and Jesus Christ, our Lord and Saviour.
We are told to love one another –
it is a commandment from God.

Printed in the United States
By Bookmasters